MEDIATION ADVOCACY
Nigeria Edition

Discourage litigation. Persuade your neighbours to compromise whenever you can. Point out to them how the nominal winner is often a real loser – in fees, expenses, and waste of time. As a peacemaker the lawyer has a superior opportunity of being a good man. There will still be business enough.

Abraham Lincoln
Notes for a Law Lecture, July 1, 1850

Good lawyers must have the skills required for professional competence. But this is not enough. They must know how to carry the burdens of other people on their shoulders. They must know of pain, and how to help heal it. Lawyers can be healers. Like physicians, ministers, and other healers, lawyers are persons to whom other people open up their innermost secrets when they have suffered or are threatened with serious injury. People go to them to be healed, to be made whole, and to regain control of their lives.

James D Gordon III
Law Review and the Modern Mind
(1991) 33 Arizona L. Rev. 271

ABOUT THE AUTHOR

Andrew Goodman

Andrew Goodman has been a barrister since 1978 and an accredited CEDR mediator since 1992 practicing from chambers at 1 Chancery Lane, London in commercial, construction, partnership, franchising, professional negligence and farming disputes. He has been recommended as a leading junior in professional indemnity work and in ADR in the Legal 500 for over 15 years. He is currently Professor of Conflict Management and Dispute Resolution Studies at Rushmore University, and undertaking doctoral research in mediation dynamics at Birkbeck College, University of London, and is a visiting lecturer on the LLM/LLB Dispute Resolution programme at University College, London, and the School of Oriental and African Studies.

In November, 2007 Andrew helped launch the Standing Conference of Mediation Advocates of which he is Convenor. In that capacity he has since given training in mediation advocacy throughout the United Kingdom, and in Paris, Brussels, Ankara, Lagos, Dubai and Hong Kong. He has also advised members of the judiciary, ministries of justice and n.g.o's on the engagement of the legal profession with court-annexed mediation and top-down civil procedural codes in Belgium, Croatia, Nigeria, Ghana, UAE and the People's Republic of China.

He was requested to submit evidence to Lord Woolf's Committee on Access to Justice on Court Annexed ADR Practices in other jurisdictions, and to Lord Justice Jackson's Review of Civil Costs. He is currently a member of the Bar's ADR Committee and a Bar Council mediation advocacy trainer, and Director of RICS Accredited Mediator Training. He is deviser and course leader for the RICS APC course in Dispute Resolution and Conflict Management.

Andrew is the author and editor of over 30 books including *The Court Guide* (OUP 2006/7, 20th edn.) and *The Prison Guide* (Blackstone 1999). He wrote *The RCJ Guide* (Longman 1985) and *The Walking Guide to Lawyer's London* (OUP 2000), produced *The RCJ Plans* (Legastat 1988 onwards) and has had numerous articles published in the legal and academic press; he devised and edited *What's It Worth? Updated General Damages Awards in Non-Personal Injury Claims (Vol. 1 Property Claims)* (EMIS 2004). August, 2005 saw the publication of his seminal *How Judges Decide Cases: Reading,*

Writing and Analysing Judgments (xpl publishing), followed by its sequel *Influencing the Judicial Mind: Effective Written Advocacy in Practice* (xpl 2006). In April 2006 he established xpl-Professional Skills Training offering bespoke in-house specialist and advanced training in written advocacy and mediation representation/advocacy: see www.xpl-pst.com. He has written for *Commercial Lawyer* and appeared on Legal Network Television, Yorkshire Television, ITN News at Ten, the Discovery Channel, BBC Radio 4, Radio London, GLR and London Live, Radio Essex, Kent, Lancashire and the World Service. He has also written a number of books on late Victorian theatre and acted as a technical consultant on the Oscar-winning Mike Leigh film *Topsy-Turvy* and for a PBS documentary in the United States.

The Nigerian edition of this book is endorsed by the Standing Conference of Mediation Advocates and supports the work of the Network of Multi-Door Courthouses, and the training courses offered by those institutions and by the School of Estate, Lagos.

MEDIATION ADVOCACY
Nigeria Edition

Andrew Goodman LLB,MBA,FCIArb,FRSA
Of the Inner Temple, a Master of the Bench
Professor of Conflict Management and Dispute Resolution
Studies, Rushmore University
Convenor, Standing Conference of Mediation Advocates

Foreword by

The Hon. Mrs Justice Opeyemi O. Oke
Judge of the High Court of Lagos State and Chairman of the
Governing Council of the Lagos Multi-Door Courthouse,
Nigeria

Foreword to the UK First Edition by the
Rt. Hon Lord Justice Dyson

xpl

UK First edition © Andrew Goodman and Alastair Hammerton, 2006
Second edition © Andrew Goodman 2010
Nigeria edition © Andrew Goodman 2010

Published by

xpl publishing
99 Hatfield Road
St Albans AL1 4JL
UK

www.xplpublishing.com

Paper   ISBN 978 1 85811 707 2

Printed and typeset in the UK

Preface to the Nigeria Edition and Acknowledgments

The original purpose of the UK edition of this book, which concerns the representation of parties in mediation, has not changed since it was conceived in 2006. It was and is primarily to engage lawyers in the process and structure of mediation. However the techniques and skills that are discussed and analysed should not be confined to members of the legal profession. They ought also to extend to all those providing mediation representation, including accountants, surveyors, construction, property and human resources professionals, trade union officers and experts.

There is a clear distinction between mediation and litigation as methods of dispute resolution, whether state sanctioned or wholly in private hands, and as part of this distinction, the impact of the High Court of the Federal Capital Territory, Abuja, Civil Procedure Rules 2004 ('the FCT Rules'), the High Court of Lagos State (Civil Procedure) Rules 2004 ('the Lagos Rules'), the Lagos Multi-Door Courthouse Law 2007 ('the LMDC Law'), the LMDC Practice Direction on Mediation Procedure 2008 ('the LMDC PD'), and the Kano High Court ADR Centre MDC Bill 2009 and Protocol ('the Kano Protocol') on court-managed litigation must be taken into account. Although these rules may be unfamiliar to some non-lawyer readers, there is no apology for mentioning them because of their huge influence on the dispute-resolution landscape. Hopefully all those who appear at mediation appointments will benefit from the suggestions set out here, which are intended to be practical and drawn from experience of what is a rapidly growing, but relatively new, industry.

There ought to be far less mystique about mediation, and its processes, than the mediation service providers, those bodies that train, accredit and provide mediators, would have users believe. Whatever the reasons for such mystique, it is in the interests of users to demystify the process by writing about mediation from the advocates' point of view. Representatives need to know how properly to prepare themselves and their client for the event, what to expect on the day, and how to deal with the mediator throughout his or her appointment, and in so doing to protect their client's best interests. And they need to recognise that the skills needed for non-adversarial representation are very different from trial advocacy, yet equally valid.

Both the Hon. Justice A. Ade Alabi (Lagos) and the Hon. Justice Hassan Lawal Gummi (Abuja) have endorsed the use of ADR/mediation wherever appropriate. It is an area that can only expand, and one that will be accepted by the next generation of lawyers and other professionals managing disputes as fully part of the resolution landscape in which they are trained.

I gratefully acknowledge the generous foreword of the Hon. Mrs Justice Opeyemi O. Oke, Judge of the High Court of Lagos State and Chairman of the Governing Council of the Lagos Multi-Door Courthouse for this edition, and that of Lord Justice Dyson, as he then was, for the first UK edition, and the support and encouragement of a number of friends and colleagues in the UK. In particular I would like to thank Alastair Hammerton who co-authored the first edition of this work in the UK, Philip Bartle QC, John Burgess, Beverly-Ann Rogers, David Miles, Andrew Paton, Michael Lind of ADR Group, the members of the Advisory Board of the SCMA and the members of the ADR Committee of the General Council of the Bar of England and Wales.

I wish to express my thanks to Mr Valentino Buoro, SCMA Co-ordinator for Nigeria. Mrs Caroline Etuk, Director of LMDC ADR Centre, and her assistant, Mrs Adeyinka Aroyewun for their guidance, and for permission to reprint as an appendix the LMDC PD; and Mr S.B.Onu, General Secretary of the Nigerian Bar Association (Lagos Branch), and Mr O.C. Agbafo, Chairman of the Lagos Bar CPD Committee for their kind encouragement, and Mr Akin Olawore, Director of Studies of the Lagos School of Estate which kindly sponsored my visit to Lagos in May, 2010.

The Royal Institution of Chartered Surveyors Dispute Resolution Services and Littleton Dispute Resolution Services Ltd have kindly granted me permission to reproduce as appendices their current standard form mediation agreements, for which I thank them. I also wish to acknowledge the kind assistance of Michel Kallipetis QC in allowing me to draw from his paper on Mediation Privilege and Confidentiality which forms a substantial part of Chapter 6, and of Matthew Rushton for his original research into the mediation market which formed the basis of an article in the Mediator magazine in 2009 from which I have drawn material used in Chapter 8.

The first edition of this book started a debate among our fellow mediation advocates. The concept is gradually becoming more accepted. Training courses in advocacy in ADR are the single most important means by which members of the legal and professional community can engage with mediators trained by domestic or foreign organisations, such as NCMG, SPIDR, AFMA or CEDR and I commend this book to the students of such courses. Any constructive criticism, which is entirely welcome, can be directed to agoodman@1chancerylane.com

Andrew Goodman
1 Chancery Lane
London WC2A 1LF
August, 2010.

FOREWORD

I have observed the development of Alternative Dispute Resolution (ADR) for two decades, from the early 1990's when the Lagos Multi-Door Courthouse (LMDC) was established as the first court-connected ADR Centre in Africa to the present. Therefore, I can attest to the fact that there has been a gradual but progressive change of attitude to ADR which demonstrates the increasing acceptability of this concept as a viable supplement to litigation. However, this progress in the right direction has not been without objections from the Legal Community, Judiciary and other Stakeholders and certain other cultural factors which have characterized the growth of ADR in other jurisdictions of the world.

Passion and industry have been the twin forces that have driven the vehicle of reform. Government support to key ADR institutions and the legislative imprimatur which has established a legal framework for the practice of ADR has brought its development further up the road. In Lagos State the support of the Judiciary and its involvement in court-connected initiatives has proved to be a key to the more recent impetus to this movement. These developments have caught the attention of International funding agencies particularly in the area of commercial ADR intervention strategies. Other programmes, like the first settlement week in Nigeria which was organized by the LMDC in November 2009 and which has become part of the Judicial Calendar of the Lagos State Judiciary, have become a model for replication throughout the Federation. The widespread training of mediators and the establishment of ADR organizations have also become commonplace in the dispute resolution landscape.

This Nigerian Edition of *Mediation Advocacy* is a welcome intervention in the evolution of our dispute resolution jurisprudence. Professor Andrew Goodman's text has made its debut at a critical time in the history of our Judiciary and its promise will no doubt influence the course of ADR growth in a remarkably positive way. For one, it will promote the inter-disciplinary practice of mediation advocacy and create a corps of mediation promoters and advisors to take the movement to the next level. Indeed the much desired 'culture' change in dispute resolution now appears within arms' grasp.

It is my earnest hope that this publication will challenge traditional stereotypical views and approaches which view justice administration as the exclusive preserve of the legal professional while serving as a demand on the legal community to embrace the new thinking in justice delivery as a matter of professionalism, social service and profitability.

Hon. Justice Opeyemi O. Oke (Mrs.),
Judge of the High Court of Lagos State and
Chairman of the Governing Council of the Lagos Multi-Door Courthouse,
Nigeria.

FOREWORD TO THE UK FIRST EDITION

The importance of mediation is now generally well understood. Any proportionate means of avoiding the stress and expense of litigation is to be encouraged. Court-based mediation schemes are springing up throughout the country. There are growing numbers of mediation providers. The Civil Procedure Rules and the Protocols emphasise that parties should always consider whether the case is suitable for mediation. The courts are now enjoined to order the parties to consider mediation. Costs sanctions may be imposed if a party unreasonably refuses to participate in a mediation. No longer is it acceptable for a judge to regard mediation as being of no concern to him or her. The climate has changed, and with remarkable speed.

That is why the publication of this book is so timely. Lawyers are now expected to advise their clients about the benefits of mediation and, where appropriate, represent them before mediators. There is no shortage of opportunity for training mediators. But advocates also have an important part to play if the potential of mediation is to be fully realised. The advocacy skills necessary in a mediation are quite different from those required for the (usually civilised) battle that takes place in a courtroom. That is why *Mediation Advocacy* is such a valuable book. It gives a great deal of very useful advice as to how to prepare for and conduct a mediation from beginning to end. It is an intensely practical book. It will be of great benefit to all those who conduct litigation.

Rt Hon Lord Justice Dyson
March 2006

CONTENTS

GLOSSARY

ABA	American Bar Association
ADMC	Abuja Multi-Door Courthouse
ADMC PD	Abuja Multi-Door Courthouse Practice Direction 2007
ADR Judge	Judge of the High Court of Lagos State appointed to carry out the activities and functions contained in the LMDC PD
AFMA	African Mediation Association
AIM	American Institute of Mediation
CEDR	Centre for Effective Dispute Resolution
DRO	Dispute Resolution Officer
FCT Rules	High Court of the Federal Capital Territory (Civil Procedure) Rules 2004
KMDC	Kanu Multi-Door Courthouse
KMDCH	Kaduna Multi-Door Courthouse
Lagos Rules	High Court of Lagos (Civil Procedure) Rules 2004
LMDC	Lagos Multi-Door Courthouse
LMDC Law	A Law to Establish the Lagos Multi-Door Courthouse and Connected Matters 2007/21
LMDC PD	LMDC Practice Direction on Mediation Procedure 2007
MDCs	Multi-Door Courthouses at Lagos, Abuja, Kano, Kaduna, Abia, Akwa Ibom and Delta States
MSME	Micro, Small and Medium Enterprises
NCMG	Negotiation and Conflict Management Group
NCMG Rules	NCMG Centre for Dispute Resolution Rules 2002
NIPC	Nigerian Investment Promotion Commission
NMDC	Network of Multi-Door Courthouses
SCMA	Standing Conference of Mediation Advocates
SPIDR	Society of Professionals in Dispute Resolution

Table of Cases

Introduction

Mediation is not a soft option for the advocate. The skills required may be equally forensic, but they are very different from what is needed in the court room or at trial. They have a subtlety that needs to be addressed. If you are unprepared, if you do not know what to expect, if you do not know what you are doing, your client will be at a considerable disadvantage and you will come unstuck.

This book is aimed at lawyers and other professional advocates who represent clients in mediation. It is written not only for "first-timers" needing to learn about the basics of mediation very quickly, particularly as to what they should expect and how they should prepare, but also for those more seasoned advocates wishing to specialise in mediation advocacy and who want to develop the particular skills that it requires. The present edition also reflects the growing need to educate a younger generation of lawyers that mediation is not an alien or even unusual process, or one incompatible with other forms of dispute processing. In choosing the most appropriate outcome for the client, mediation is merely another tool to be used by the informed professional, who therefore needs to understand how to use the process to optimise his client's interests.

Specialist advocacy in mediation is still in its infancy but there is no reason to suppose that, as court-annexed schemes develop and mediation comes to be regarded as just another form of dispute resolution hearing in which representation is required, the advocate's particular expertise should not be developed so that mediation advocacy becomes a desirable specialist skill.

There has been a clear move in recent years away from the generalist mediator to the lawyer specialist mediator or neutral. It has been recognised by sophisticated commercial parties with complex disputes that lawyer mediators with expertise in the field of the dispute give mediation a better chance of success. Informed commercial parties look for sensible reasons, based on proper risk analysis of the litigation in question, to found a recommendation for settlement. They settle because there are sound commercial reasons for doing so, usually based, at least in substantial part, on a careful analysis of the strengths and weaknesses of the case.[1] All this has an impact on the responsibility of the legal or other representative. He has a specific role and must be thoroughly prepared. This

---

[1] *New Sophistications in Commercial Mediation*, Elizabeth Birch, ACI newsletter issue 9 Spring/Summer 2004.

book is designed to help prepare advocates to use the mediation process to their and their clients' best advantage.

The Growth in Mediation

In recent years the use of mediation has increased exponentially across the world. The European Directive on Mediation in Civil and Commercial Matters[2] has been implemented and EU governments must effect compliance by 21 May, 2011. Court-annexed or court-regulated mediation has now become widely accepted in such jurisdictions as Belgium, The Netherlands, Rumania, Bulgaria, Germany, Croatia, Slovenia, the UAE and Hong Kong where a mediation practice direction under the recent Civil Justice Rules came into effect on 1st January 2010. China, India and many African countries are striving to train commercial mediators, which they will need in large numbers.

In Nigeria the Federal and State authorities recognised more than ten years ago that the civil justice system was not coping with the demands of modern litigants. Delay and cost were in particular causing foreign corporations and investors in Nigerian industry and natural resources to look elsewhere for processes to resolve their commercial disputes by ADR at a time when no infrastructure existed to keep such work in Nigeria.

The Negotiation and Conflict Management Group (NCMG) initiated the Multi-Door Courthouse concept in Nigeria in collaboration with the High Court of Lagos, and established the Lagos Multi-Door Courthouse (LMDC) in June, 2002. After its inception NCMG administered the LMDC under the NCMG Centre for Dispute Resolution Rules as a private-public sector partnership. The Multi-Door concept refers to the various options available at first, to the LMDC, and since, elsewhere, to consider appropriate dispute resolution routes including mediation, arbitration, early neutral evaluation and hybrids of these.

In May, 2007 an enabling law was passed in Lagos State, now known as the LMDC Law, as a consequence of which the NCMG Rules were replaced by the LMDC Practice Direction on Mediation Procedure 2007 which remains the substantive operating procedure, and which has been annexed by kind permission as an appendix to this book.[3] The LMDC Law provides a model for ADR Bills now under consideration in Kano, Kaduna and elsewhere.

NCMG was also instrumental in establishing the Abuja Multi-Door Courthouse (AMDC) on October 13, 2003, which operates its own Practice

---

[2] Directive 2008/52/EC 21 May 2008.
[3] See p.187.

Direction under the supervisory jurisdiction of the High Court of the Federal
Capital Territory (Civil Procedure) Rules 2004.

Lagos and Abuja MDCs were the breakthrough institutions in providing
ADR services, and there is currently a bid to replicate the same system in all
the states of the Federation. Kano, Kaduna, Abia, and Akwa Ibom have since
joined the elite league of judiciaries with court connected ADR centres. The
government of Delta State recently established an ADR Centre known as the
Department of People's Rights in the Ministry of Justice, which is operated
by the Institute for Dispute Resolution.

For international disputes, the Regional Centre for International Commercial
Arbitration[4] provides high-quality services to the entire West African region.
The public-private partnership is growing in Nigeria, with the LMDC as
prime example. Private law firms also offer services in ADR, supplementing
the institutional services provided.

The Multi-Door Courthouses maintain a panel of Neutrals made up of
reputable professionals and retired judges trained for ADR proceedings. In
2009 the Nigerian Investment Promotion Commission (NIPC) acting as an
executing agency of the World Bank, embarked with NCMG and ADR
Centre (Italy) on a programme of research, public awareness, training for
lawyers and training for trainers to promote ADR among Micro, Small and
Medium Enterprises. In addition UK, American and Canadian organisations
regularly promote mediation training and awareness in Nigeria.

In most ADR Centres when a case comes, either on a court-directed basis or
a walk-in basis, the parties are requested to submit their Statement of Issues
– which is a summary of the main facts of their disputes. Upon receipt the
ADR Registrar exchanges the statements between the parties and invites
them for a preliminary meeting or screening.[5]

The facts of the case are screened by an experienced Dispute Resolution Officer
(DRO) who selects the appropriate door he or she believes to be suitable for the
resolution of the dispute and invites the parties for a pre-session conference to
inform them of the Door proposed to be utilized and the procedures involved in
the settlement. The pre-session begins with an explanation of the programme
and a review of the protocol including confidentiality. The parties then make
short and formal presentations of their perspectives on the legal foundation of
the case; legal damages or equitable relief sought; and any other procedural

[4] Also located in Lagos.
[5] www.amdcng.net

matters. In this non-adversarial setting, the parties are usually able to hear each other's perspectives in a less defensive manner. Sometimes a common ground and the basis for further settlement discussions are established at this time. In addition, the screener tries to elicit information about subjective, non-legal issues, in a bid to reach the real issues to be determined.

The next meeting to be agreed upon is for a session meeting where hopefully their disputes would be resolved.

It is of crucial importance that the parties attend the sessions in person to maximize the effectiveness of the process. Lawyers may accompany their clients, however parties cannot dispense with appearing at the session by sending their lawyers. Failure to attend can give rise to an immediate financial penalty or later costs sanction.

Parties attending ADR sessions must have full authority, which must be in writing, to settle the dispute in order for the session to proceed. The ADR session may be cancelled if the attending party lacks the requisite authority.

Parties are at liberty to choose one or more from among the list of neutrals for the purpose of the ADR process. It is instructive to note that the composition of the Panel of Neutrals is not limited to lawyers but extends to accountants, bankers and other professionals, including the property, construction and energy industries.

The LMDC Law sets out statutory objectives, namely to

(a) enhance access to justice by providing alternative mechanisms to supplement litigation in the resolution of disputes;

(b) minimize citizen frustration and delays in justice delivery by providing a standard legal framework for fair and efficient settling of disputes through ADR;

(c) serve as the focal point for the promotion of ADR in Lagos State, and

(d) promote the growth and effective functioning of the justice system through ADR methods.

The powers of LMDC extend to applying ADR mechanisms to disputes referred to it from the High Court of Justice, Lagos State, courts of other jurisdictions, Federal courts, private persons or corporations, public institutions and dispute resolution organisations.

The Federal Government of Nigeria has recognised the value of mediation and sought to increase its use, urging MDCs to increase the take-up generally of the many services provided. In the present legal landscape it is therefore essential both for all lawyers, and any others representing parties to a dispute, to have a good understanding of the mediation process. The use of mediation is certainly not the sole prerogative of the legal profession. This book is therefore aimed at helping all those involved.

Let us therefore start with the basics.

What is Mediation?

Mediation is a voluntary, non-binding, and private dispute resolution process in which a (trained) neutral person helps the parties try to reach a negotiated settlement.[6]

Voluntary

In most cases mediation cannot take place unless the parties agree to enter the process, although this may only be after a strong judicial recommendation, with an associated risk of cost sanctions against a party who refuses to mediate and indeed a fine for parties who do not attend the hearing before the ADR Judge to determine the appropriate route[7]. Mediation is not possible without the participation of all parties, and will cease if one party walks out, which they are free to do at any time.

Non-binding

Mediation is also truly voluntary, as entering the process does not bind the parties to reaching settlement; unlike arbitral dispute resolution processes, mediation cannot be continued by the opposite party should your client choose to leave the process. Settlement can only come about on the authority of the parties concerned. As the mediator has no authority to make a binding determination, if the parties cannot agree, then there will be no settlement and the case will proceed to the next stage in the litigation process. However, if settlement is reached the agreed terms will, in the private sector form part of an enforceable contract, and under most court-annexed schemes will become an enforceable judgment of the High Court.[8]

Private

Although refusing to mediate can have adverse costs consequences, the mediation process is both "without prejudice" and absolutely confidential to

---

[6] See Brown and Marriot, *ADR Principles and Practice*, 2nd Edition, Sweet and Maxwell 1999, 127-131.
[7] E.g. Article 13b) LMDC PD.
[8] *Njoku v Ikeeuchu* (1972) 2 ECSLR 199 per Ikpeazu J.; s.19 LMDC Law and Article 17 LMDC PD; Ord 39 r4(3) High Court of Lagos (Civil Procedure) Rules 2004; s.11 Sheriff and Civil Process Law.

the extent the law permits.[9] This means that parties can conduct themselves in the mediation, for example by disclosing information, expressing views, making suggestions or offering concessions, safe in the knowledge that this will not preclude them arguing a different position should the matter proceed to trial. Similarly, a party is free to refuse offers made in mediation, or even to walk out, without the risk of this being held against them if a court determines costs in the future.[10] The confidential nature of mediation negotiations stands in clear contrast to the courtroom, which is in public and potentially extremely embarrassing. Of course, should mediation break down a party is free to formalise an offer made during mediation as an offer which would carry the usual costs implications.

The terms of any settlement agreed in mediation are usually also confidential. However, this need not necessarily be so. In certain disputes one of the parties may be seeking some kind of public vindication (e.g. in a defamation case) or apology for past conduct and there is no reason why a public declaration cannot form part of a mediated settlement.

Neutral Mediator

The parties' faith in the mediator is key to the success of any mediation, and it is essential that the advocate knows how to select the best person for the job and work with him or her. The mediator must be a truly neutral person having no association with either of the parties nor any interest in the outcome. Mediation requires all parties to trust and give authority to the mediator. Should any party withdraw that authority, the mediation will come to an end. Likewise, should trust in the mediator be broken for any reason, it is unlikely that a settlement will be reached.

The mediator's role is to assist the parties in their negotiations with each other and help the parties work towards a consensual resolution of the dispute. However, the parties themselves remain responsible for their own decisions and answerable for the terms of any settlement that may be agreed.

A settlement, negotiated by the parties

As highlighted above, a settlement is only possible in mediation with the consent

---

[9] See Article 15 LMDC PD *Farm Assist Ltd (in Liquidation) v DEFRA (No.2)* [2009] EWHC 1102 (TCC). *Venture Investment Placement Ltd v Hall* [2005] EWHC 1227 (Ch) and *Reed Executive Plc v Reed Business Information* [2004] EWCA Civ 887 applying *Rush & Tompkins Ltd v GLC* [1989] AC 1280 HL but cf *In Re a Company* [2005] EWHC 3317 (Ch) where what occurred in the mediation was the subject of satellite litigation.
[10] See *Halsey* op.cit and *Burchell v Bullard* [2005] EWCA Civ 358.

of the parties, and it is they who are responsible for the terms of any agreement. While mediation certainly aims for a resolution that maximises all parties' interests (often called "win-win" outcomes), by its very nature it should never achieve an outcome with which one party cannot live. As the onus of arriving at the terms of settlement rests with the parties, the flexibility of the process allows for more ingenuity and extra-legal solutions than would ever be possible from a determination imposed by a court or other arbitral process. This responsibility also offers party empowerment, and frees participants from having to think in terms of cause of action and available remedy.

When mediation might be inappropriate

Since the courts are likely now to impose sanctions on a party who unreasonably fails to mediate, this begs the question when is it reasonable to refuse mediation, or in which cases is mediation inappropriate?

This issue was considered in *Halsey v Milton Keynes General NHS Trust* [2004] EWCA Civ 576; [2004] 1 WLR 3002 where the England and Wales Court of Appeal was more sympathetic to parties who refuse to mediate than Lightman J had been in the earlier case of *Hurst v Leeming* [2002] EWHC 1051 (Ch); [2003] 1 Lloyd's Rep 37. In that case, Lightman J suggested that to escape a sanction for refusal, the refusing party would have to show that mediation would have no reasonable prospect of success. In *Halsey* the Court of Appeal took a more subtle approach: the starting point is that to deprive a successful party of all or part of its costs, (or, presumably, to impose a sanction on an unsuccessful party) the other side must show he has behaved unreasonably in failing to mediate.

Dyson LJ considered that a number of factors should be taken into consideration when assessing whether a party behaved unreasonably, and these included:[11]

- The nature of the dispute;
- The merits of the case;
- The extent to which other settlement methods have been attempted
- Whether the costs of the mediation would be disproportionately high;
- Whether any delay in setting up and attending the mediation would have been prejudicial; and
- Whether the mediation had a reasonable prospect of success.

---

[11] At [17]-[24].

Dyson LJ acknowledged that a small number of cases are intrinsically unsuitable for mediation, and gave a number of examples of these [12]

> (1) Where the parties wish the court to determine issues of law or construction which may be essential to the future trading relations of the parties, as under an on-going long term contract, or where the issues are generally important for those participating in a particular trade or market

> (2) Similarly, where a party wants the court to resolve a point of law that arises from time to time, and one or more parties consider that a binding precedent would be useful.

> (3) Cases involving allegations of fraud or other disreputable conduct against an individual or group, which are unlikely to be successfully mediated because confidence is lacking in the future conduct of that party.

> (4) Cases where injunctive or other relief is essential to protect the position of a party.

The judge went on to consider that where a party actually does have a watertight case, a refusal to mediate can be reasonable, pointing out that otherwise there would be scope for parties with a weak case to use the threat of a costs sanction to force a party into a mediated settlement even where the claim or defence is without merit. However, the party's belief that his case is watertight must be reasonable.

The Court of Appeal held that the costs of mediation can be a factor of particular importance where the sums at stake in the litigation are small. This is because a mediation can sometimes be as expensive as a day in court, as the parties will often have legal representation and the mediator's fees and other disbursements are usually be borne equally by the parties regardless of the outcome. In addition the possibility of the ultimately successful party being required to incur the costs of an abortive mediation is a relevant factor that a court may take into account in deciding whether the successful party acted unreasonably in refusing to agree to ADR/mediation.

This is an important consideration bearing in mind the increasing trend for courts to suggest mediation in small claims. Remember, mediation is not a

---

[12] At [18].

panacea. *For a legally represented client, a small claims mediation is likely to cost at least the same as the hearing itself, but with no guarantee of an outcome at the end of it.* An unsuccessful mediation in a small claim will effectively double a legally represented client's costs, whether or not this client is eventually successful.

When considering whether mediation stood any reasonable prospect of success, the Court of Appeal in *Halsey*, in contrast to *Hurst v Leeming*, held that the burden was on the party seeking to prove the other side had behaved unreasonably to show that mediation would have had a reasonable prospect of success.

The Benefits of Mediation

Facts and figures for the effectiveness of mediation are limited since by and large the outcome remains confidential, and in some cases the existence of both dispute and mediation is also confidential – one of its benefits. Member courts of the Network of Multi-Door Courthouses keep a record of cases for the purpose of state High Court statistics. It must also be recognised that there is a body of entirely unreported mediation activity, although not yet sizeable in Nigeria. Anecdotal evidence from those involved in mediation suggests that a very high proportion of mediated cases do settle at the mediation appointment, with a further considerable proportion settling soon afterwards. For example, the Centre for Effective Dispute Resolution ("CEDR"), a UK mediation service provider training organisation that makes regular visits to both LMDC and AMDC, reports on its website that over 70% of cases referred to it settle.

In addition to its success rate and the scope for potential cost savings, mediation has other benefits of which you should be aware when called upon to explain these to your client. Such benefits can best be seen merely by comparing traditional litigation with ADR in general, and mediation in particular.

Litigation is formal. It imposes a binding solution where inevitably one party or the other is likely to be dissatisfied with the outcome, often highly dissatisfied, since the process is designed to attribute blame. The expense and costs regime may make even the winner dissatisfied. It removes control of the dispute from parties, first by vesting it in the lawyers and then in the court's administration and management system. It addresses issues in a purely legal context, in the public eye, with fixed pre-determined remedies that you either obtain or fail to obtain. It is slow, expensive, and destroys relationships.

By contrast ADR/mediation is an informal, very flexible procedure with no imposed solutions. It gives better and more supple results because control remains directly in the hands of the parties as decision makers. Win or lose, it is comparatively quick and cheap as a self-contained process. It saves management time. It is private and confidential. And as a dynamic it actively promotes renewal and reconciliation because it is designed to restore relationships.

Litigation looks to find fault. Mediation does not. This makes mediation a particularly attractive route where parties are likely to continue to have dealings and to interact in the future, whether in business, as neighbours or within the confines of some close personal relationship or physical proximity.

In *Halsey* the Court of Appeal also took the opportunity to promote the advantages of mediation:

> "We recognise that mediation has a number of advantages over the court process. It is usually less expensive than litigation which goes all the way to judgment.... Mediation provides litigants with a wider range of solutions than those that are available in litigation: for example, an apology; an explanation; the continuation of an existing professional or business relationship perhaps on new terms; and an agreement by one party to do something without any existing legal obligation to do so."[13]

ADR, and in particular mediation, is here to stay. All litigators must have a basic understanding of its principles and practice to be able to act in an advisory role. As advisers, you must be able to identify cases, both pre-and mid-proceedings, for which mediation is appropriate, and to explain the mediation process to both your clients and their supporters, and to other legal professionals. As advocates, you must be able to prepare cases for mediation in a manner that best represents the client's interests, and to engage in strategies that will ensure their clients' cases are presented as effectively as possible. The adversarial approach in mediation is very different to that used in litigation. You must not kick against it, but learn to recognise the value of the mediation process as a legitimate and routine method of case management and disposal.

---

[13] Op.cit. @[15].

PART 1

The Role of the Advocate in Mediation

Chapter 1

1.1 The Role of the Advocate in Mediation: The Wider Context

The development of modern civil/commercial mediation practice over the past twenty years in the United Kingdom and six or so in Nigeria, and the ideologies underpinning mediation, reflect both the changing attitudes of disputants, and the ebb and flow of state intervention in the delivery of civil justice as a response to market forces over those periods. In particular in state jurisdiction throughout Nigeria it is recognised that the civil justice system is slow, expensive and may not serve the true interests of the parties as consumers.

However what was once intended as a flexible, procedure-free (and, to an extent, lawyer-free), unregulated   dispute processing method, has been the subject of increasing juridification (or 'law creep') over the last six or seven years as state endorsement or sponsorship of mediation has increased. In the UK courts have busied themselves with examining the enforceability of mediation clauses,[1] the extent of confidentiality and privilege attaching to the process,[2] the enforceability of mediated settlement agreements,[3] and the liability of participants and non-parties when things go wrong.[4] In this jurisdiction the FCT, Lagos and Kano Multi-Door courthouses are interventionist in promoting the use of ADR in existing litigation. The mediation practitioner must therefore at least be aware of the existence of a growing body of authority attaching to the mediation process.

The impact of the EU Directive on Mediation[5] and the harmonisation of pan-European mediation practice will inevitably lead to regulation of the 'industry' if not the 'profession' of mediator in the next few years. The joined-up approach of the Network of Multi-Door Courthouses with regard to education and training, practice and ethics suggests that this may be no bad thing in Nigeria.

---

[1] *Balfour Beatty Construction Northern Ltd* v *Modus Corovest (Blackpool) Ltd* [2008] EWHC 3029 TCC.
[2] *Farm Assist Ltd (in Liquidation)* v *DEFRA (No.2)* [2009] EWHC 1102 (TCC).
[3] *Vedatech Corpn* v *Crystal Decision UK Ltd and Crystal Decision (Japan) KK* [2003] EWCA Civ 1066; see also Foskett QC, David *The Law and Practice of Compromise* Thomson Sweet & Maxwell 6th Edn 2005 4-37/4-50.
[4] E.g. *In Re a Company* [2005] EWHC 3317 (Ch).
[5] Directive 2008/52/EC 21 May 2008.

Thus the work of the professional advocate in mediation, using primarily the facilitative model in commercial claims, and his or her relationship with the lay client, needs to be addressed in the context of a changing law market.

1.2 The Adjudicative Model and the Historic Professional Psyche

The adjudicative or arbitral model, in all its forms, is seen historically as the core element of dispute processing, giving rise to both a cultural icon (the trial) and a social structure. The courts are seen as decision-makers, bureaucracies, instruments of state control, keepers of social norms and records, and a mechanism for applying uniform inherited patterns of authority, reflected in the acknowledgment of enforceable rights and obligations and the need for the enforcement and execution of awards and judgments. Academics[6] suggest that in the ecology of dispute processing the adjudicative process is a core phenomena because it is the most frequent symbol exemplifying shared or dominant values and therefore is a source of legitimacy for norms, offices, and acts; it is also the primary source of legal scholarship in common-law systems.

By being so, the professional education of nearly all advocates focuses on the adjudication prototype as the primary form of dispute processing. Here the norm is for representatives to present proofs and arguments to an impartial, authoritative third party decision-maker who gives a binding decision conferring a remedy or award on the basis of a pre-existing general rule.

Mediation in all its forms is a departure from the adjudication model. It offers party control and non-lawyerly or other professional language. Because it is not confined by a formal structure the dispute process has a wider relevance; and the decision is not based on rule-making since it is mediative and not arbitral, in the sense that an agreed outcome is fundamental. It impacts upon the parties as a therapeutic reintegration of their relationship based on compromise and the readjustment of their interests through shared gains. Transformative mediation[7]

---

[6] Galanter, Marc. Adjudication, Litigation and Related Phenomena, ch 4 from *Law and the Social Sciences* Lipson L., and Wheeler S., editors 1986 Russell Sage Foundation; Galanter, Marc. Compared to What? Assessing the Quality of Dispute Processing (1989) 66:3 Denver University Law Review xi : Reports of the University of Wisconsin Dispute Processing Research Program Workshop on *'Identifying and Measuring the Quality of Dispute Resolution Processes and Outcomes'*, Madison, July 13 and 14, 1987; Damaska, Mirjan R. *The Faces of Justice and State Authority* YUP 1986.
[7] Folger J. and Bush R.B. *The Promise of Mediation: Responding to Conflict Through Empowerment and Recognition* 2nd edn 2006 Jossey-Bass, San Francisco; Schwerin, Edward W.

harnesses the energy generated by the dispute and transforms the process into a problem-solving exercise.

Unlike the court structure, informal mediation offers not only the promise of accessibility of language and form, but direct lay participation, privacy, no binding-outcome, and innovative solutions.

For the present and immediate past generation of lawyers, and particularly advocates, who have been programmed that their prime function is to prove their client's case and disprove that of their opponent, the mediation process comes as an enormous jolt to their professional psyche.

To them, disputes, even if referred to a mediation process, are still regarded as bi-polar. Thus a complaining party who claims an infringement of his rights based on social norms, seeks a remedy against a party who is the subject of complaint. Mobilisation of the complaint, or case, at the initiative of the parties requires a forum for the dispute to be processed. Participation is through expert intermediaries (lawyers with exclusive rights of audience) presenting evidence in support of requisite proofs and arguments. Disputants will expect there to be a forum that presides over a set of pre-existing forms to which it is committed – statutes and precedent. In arbitral form the repertoire of legal concepts has a narrow scope of relevance, and claims are assessed in the light of some bounded body of authoritative learning to which the forum is committed in advance.

Even more rigid than this is the element of state control: the prototypical adjudicative institution is an organ of government, located in a public building, staffed by state officers who apply public norms, and its sanctions are imposed by the compulsory powers of the state. Courts are coercive rather than voluntary since they impose outcomes regardless of the assent of the parties. This leads to a strong preponderance of claimant victories where the parties are content to have claims fought all the way to trial, since once the process is commenced they are locked in and cannot leave without either the sanction of costs or their opponent continuing to judgment without them. Settlement tends to be as a result of the threat of the coercive powers of the court, often in effect capitulation by one party.

Lawyers create and defend *interests*, and *the perception of interests*, values and norms by the use of frames of reference; disputants use them to sustain beliefs, rationalise their self-interest, convince a broader audience of the rightness of their position and generate expectation of or have preference for specific outcomes.

Therefore the ideological movement from adjudication to a flexible, client-empowered mediation process is particularly difficult for the lawyer. In facilitative mediation lawyers are generally drawn towards evaluation, since

Mediation, Citizen Empowerment and Transformational Politics 1995 Praeger, Westport, Connecticut; Burgess, Heidi *Transformative Mediation* 1997 Conflict Research Consortium.

they cannot be unaffected by their underlying structures of beliefs, values and experiences, underpinned by their professional education, which characterise their initial approach to a disputant's rights and obligations under the law.

This can be shown in the simplest of forms in Figure 1 overleaf.

Figure 1: Relationship between the Legal Case,
the Client's Story and the Client's True Needs and Interests

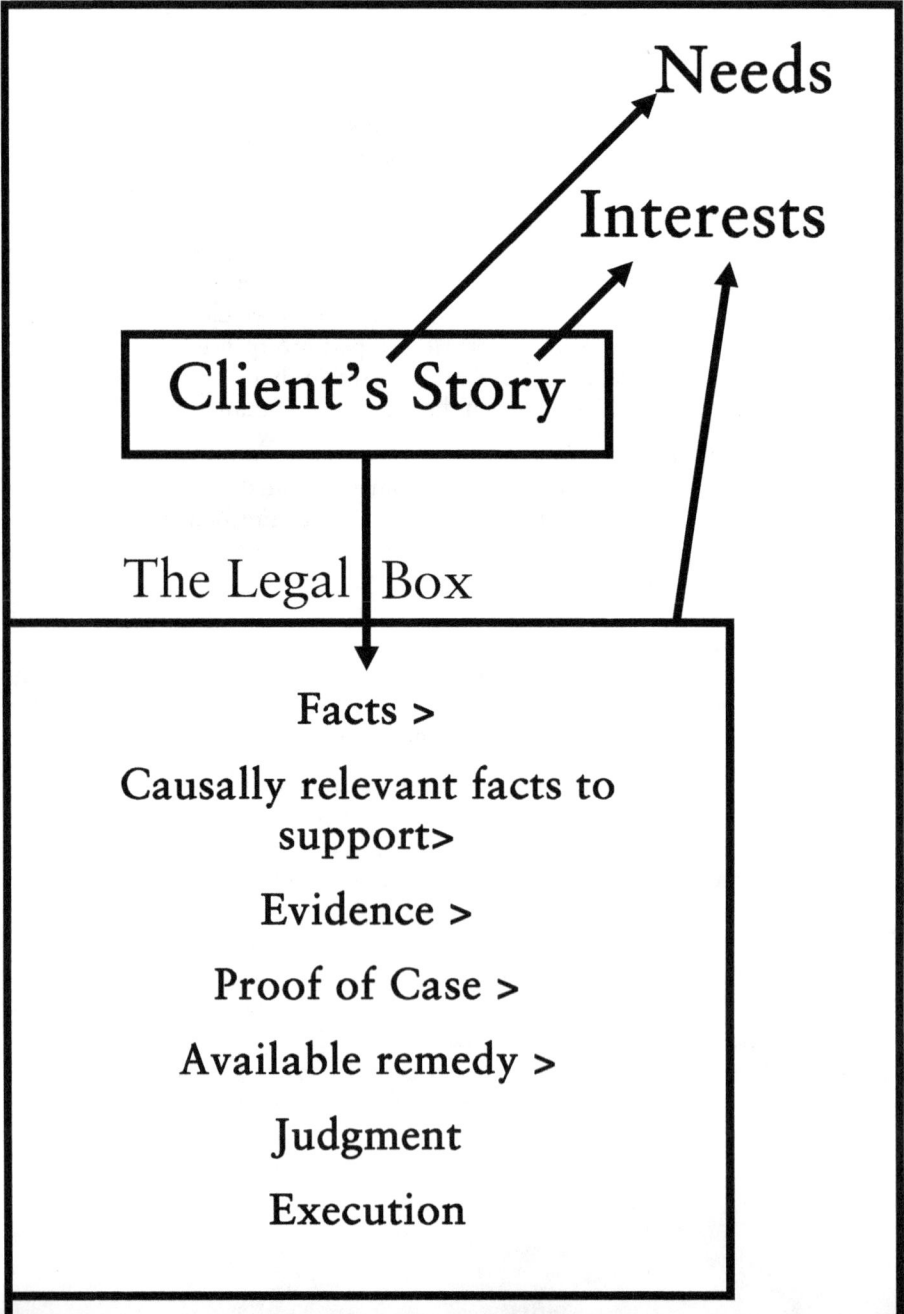

Needs

Interests

Client's Story

The Legal Box

Facts >

Causally relevant facts to support>

Evidence >

Proof of Case >

Available remedy >

Judgment

Execution

A client attends his attorney's office. He has a problem which he presents in the form of his story. The lawyer is obliged by the litigation process to distil from the facts presented only the material needed: causally relevant facts, i.e. those going to establish a legal cause of action or a defence. The lawyer is not concerned in terms of outcome with anything other than what the court process can provide by way of a remedy, or what can be negotiated with an adversary. He or she then focuses on compiling the evidence needed to prove the case and to assess and manage the risk of running the case to trial, particularly in terms of cost effectiveness under the relevant High Court Rules. The client's wider interests, for example his need for all of his story to be heard, for recognition, empathy, emotional release, catharsis and closure, may be addressed by a solicitor with a good bedside manner, but these items are not usually catered for by the litigation process or the court hearing a disposal of the claim.

For the purpose of Fig,1 the standard lawyer's role can be confined to the box entitled 'The Legal Box' to which I will refer simply as 'the Box'.

The contents of the Box leads inevitably to

- lawyer control of the claim or defence,
- the use of professional standards, language and jargon, unfamiliar to the lay client
- an uncertain fee liability for the client
- the giving away of management of the claim to the court
- the inability of the client to leave the process without either a costs sanction or worse – the right of the other side to continue in his absence
- the uncertainty of outcome, both in terms of the eventual result, its true value to the client or its relevance to the client's true needs.

The potential for conflict between the client's true needs and the litigator's services tends to make lawyers defensive about their fees, about the procedure adopted, the litigation timetable, and the outcome. In so doing they embrace the client to the extent that he is locked into a system, or indeed captured within the Box. Most practitioners, even the most client-friendly and cost-conscious, are likely to recognise the existence of these problems.

The mediation process, by contrast, is interested in the whole of the client's story, and adopts a holistic approach to problem solving, rather than the bi-lateral polarisation which is concerned with 'winning' and 'losing' cases. The mediator is intent on uncovering the parties' true needs and interests, and any underlying difficulties which have impacted on their relationship should there be one to try and restore, see Fig.2 opposite. The mediator encourages parties to speak for themselves, to use no professional language or technical jargon other than that concerned with the subject matter of the dispute, and to find and subscribe to their own solutions.

Lawyers who are inexperienced in this process find that it impacts directly on what they believe their function to be: to protect the client and advance his interests according to the strength of his legal case. In effect to lock him inside the Box.

They fail to understand that the legal case does not have to be proven in mediation, and is there to be examined principally as a frame of reference to be considered, either if things go wrong and there is no acceptable settlement, or to measure any proposal against what might occur afterwards if the case has to go to court.

The advocate therefore has a very different role, which, as we shall see later in this book, is multi-faceted and not concerned merely to be the professional leading mouthpiece. Much of what he is concerned to do is to help the client evaluate his position outside the Box, comparing and contrasting the matters within to the client's wider interests and needs outside.

1.3 Why then, use a lawyer as an advocate in mediation?

The answer lies in (i) the skill set of the lawyer advocate; (ii) the diminishing reality of empowerment; and (iii) the shadow of the law, if not the annexing of private ordering to the court process.

(i) Lawyering skills

The handicap of the lawyer's professional training and psyche is counterbalanced by his innate skills as an exponent of critical analysis, of problem solving and of communication in circumstances where dynamic change is part of the dispute process and has to be reacted to and catered for. The lawyer is trained in absorbing and processing information, seeing message patterns, and finding linguistic cues and socially constructed meanings. His or her analysis of the cognitive frames people use in a given conflict provides insight and better understanding of the conflict dynamics, of finding new ways of reaching agreement by clarifying the perception of issues, sharpening the parties understanding of interests, and identifying the means of viewing the subject matter differently, or at least identifying those differences which cannot be bridged and which may have to be set aside.

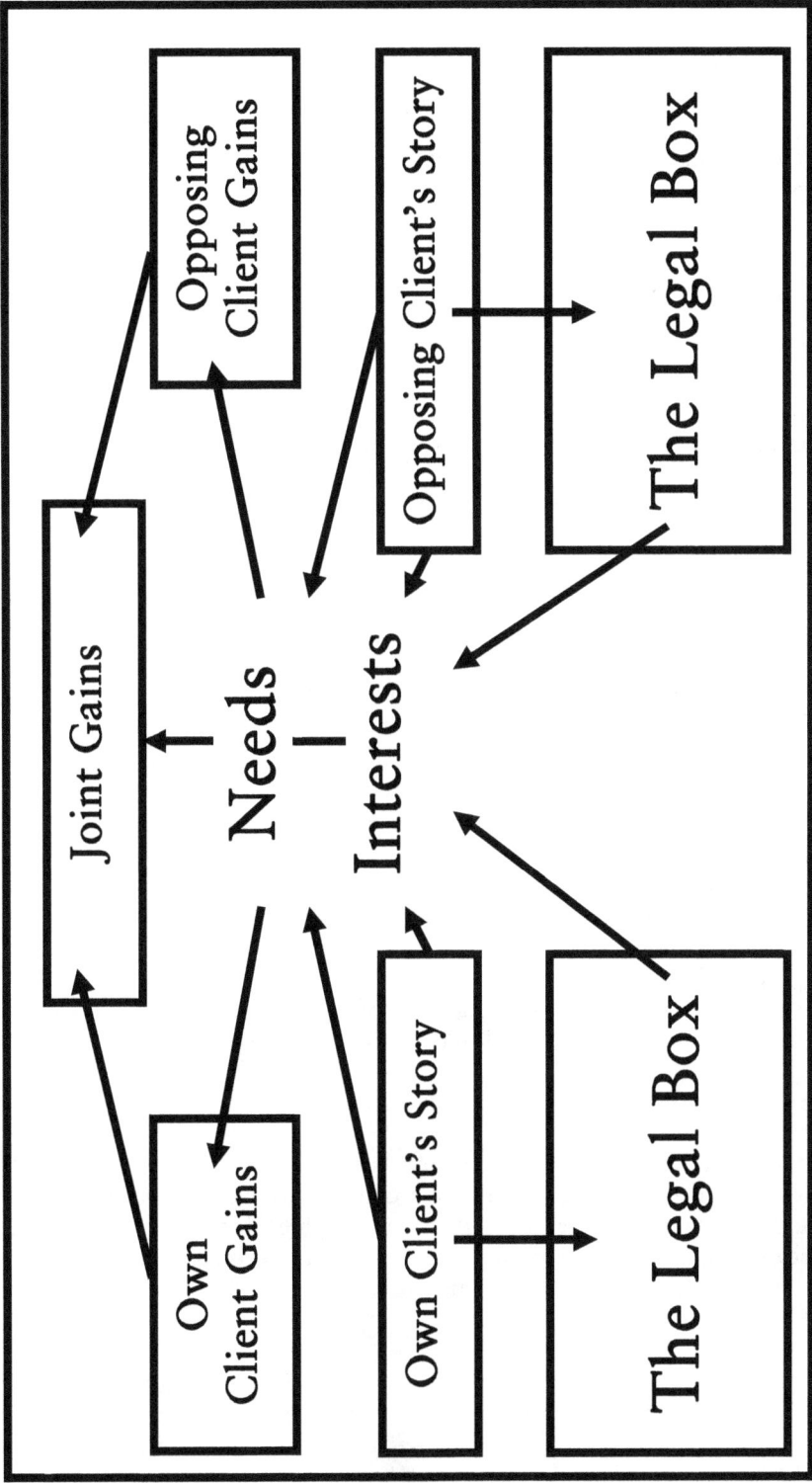

Figure 2. Mediator identifies needs and interests from both parties' stories and legal cases in order to promote individual gains and joint gains

(ii) The reality of empowerment

One of the central arguments put forward by the proponents of mediation is that it operates as a means of settling conflict that leaves responsibility for outcomes in the hands of the parties themselves, rather than have a decision imposed by a judge or reached by bargaining between partisan lawyers. Ultimately authority belongs to parties themselves.[8] However the idea of client empowerment is undermined to some extent both by the activities of the evaluative mediator and the development of a more formal structure by private sector mediation service providers, state-sponsorship in court-annexed schemes, and the extension of state activity, particularly concerning social behaviour.

This has given rise to a creeping juridification of those forms of mediation which operate within the fringes of the mainstream civil jurisdiction. In England and Wales, for example, a corpus of procedural law is taking hold of mediation in areas which concern

- Validity of the mediation agreement
- Confidentiality of the process
- The existence or otherwise of a 'mediation privilege'
- The enforceability of settlements obtained in mediation
- Mediation under actual or implicit duress by the courts.

These are problems for the advocate or party representative, and are not to be regarded as soft law, or merely matters for debate. In such areas the law actively embraces and regulates mediation practice as it would in considering its supervisory role in dealing with any other type of subordinate jurisdiction. It goes to the fundamental question of how courts view the legal nature of the mediation process, and lawyer mediation advocates will need to be able to address this issue when questioned by a judge during the case management process who wants to know about the suitability of the case for mediation.

Potentially mediation is seen by lawyers as no more than a type of procedural processing within a self-contained envelope, but one which is no less affected by the law than any other form of without-prejudice negotiation. Increasingly the 'magic' attaching to mediation as a new force in dispute processing is wearing thin.

---

[8] Folberg (1983).

(iii) The shadow of the law and court-annexed procedure

Court agendas include large portions of routine administration and supervised bargaining. Certain academics[9] have suggested that courts provide a set of "counters" to be used in bargaining between disputants. For example in divorce bargaining involves maintenance, child support, custody or residency, and matrimonial property and often one class is used to offset another. This approach is reflected in the 'Harvard model' of mediation where the concept of "bargaining endowment" is both widespread and can be seen in many complementary transactional or social relationships (husband/wife landlord/tenant purchaser/supplier) where each is based on the mutual dependence of activity.

Such counters exist within the court structure and its process – delay, cost, the uncertainty of outcome, imponderable factors such as the adequacy of proofs, exercise of the Court's discretion, the preparation of the lawyers, negotiating skills, an ability to respond to deadlines and emergencies, and an ability to recover or bear costs. These were considered by Professor Marc Galanter[10] who concluded that this bargaining between parties is a kind of "private ordering" that takes place in the shadow of the law. He suggested that the radiating effect of the courts leads to regulation within negotiation – the courts provide models (norms, procedures, structures, rationalisations) for an immense variety of regulatory settings, e.g. schools, trade unions, associations, clubs, and other host institutions which exercise regulatory authority in dispute processing to replace the expense and remoteness of the courts.

As courts have become more remote, more professional and much more expensive, they are less places for individuals to air and resolve everyday disputes and more the province of professionals and a place for the extension of government concern into areas of life previously unregulated by the state, e.g. environmental, health, safety, welfare and institutions dealing with state-dependent clients.

By the end of the 1970s shortcomings in the provision of justice were revealed, or at least perceived, in terms of cost, complexity, delay, and the separation of the law from ordinary citizens. From then onwards a jaundiced view gained ground that there was too much law and not enough justice. In England and Wales this was given credence by, among other things, the approach of Lord Denning as Master of the Rolls. This notion was, and remains, fed by the enormous growth of regulation by the state in most spheres of everyday existence. It is, however, just a popular notion since

---

[9] Mnookin & Kornhauser (1979).
[10] (1981).

studies by Galanter (2006)[11] and Menkel-Meadow (2004)[12] show a continuation of the trend identified by Abel (1982)[13] of dispute settlement less by direct decisive resolution and more by mediation, distributing bargain-counters and pattern setting. A smaller proportion of the population are direct participants in contested adjudication.

This is exemplified by statistical evidence relating to the vanishing trial, which shows the number of trials in Western common law jurisdictions have been shrinking throughout the latter part of 20th century at a time when the rest of the law is growing substantially – the amount of new laws, statutes, regulations, commentaries; the number of lawyers; the portion of GDP spent on law;[14] and legal business, all appear to have grown at a tremendous rate except for trials and definitive pronouncements of law at the highest level, by domestic Supreme Courts.

The vanishing trial is disguised by the continuing media-driven myth of the litigious society: "blame/compensation culture" makes the decline of disputes coming to trial over the last 150 years invisible to public consciousness. In particular there has been a distinct fall in the last 20 years. The process of the "day in court" has been redeemed by bargaining and shut-off points due to a huge shift in politico-judicial philosophy, the new primary role of court ('primary objective'), namely that settlement is good, judgment bad, driven by intensive case management and supported by changes in institutional practice including the withdrawal of state funding, the embrace of ADR and the outsourcing of dispute processing to other institutions.

However as Galanter (2006) remarks,[15] and to the detriment of the development of a culture of mediation, the trial holds a pivotal place in popular culture, with very little public or literary consciousness of mediation activity. What this means, for our purposes, is that at the outset of a conflict the disputant will seek the assistance and comfort of his lawyer as a hired gun, or champion, before the actual dispute procedure has been identified. Popular culture is not yet sufficiently sophisticated to recognise that mediation is not, or not necessarily, a legal process akin to a trial, and the

---

[11] Galanter, Marc *The Privatisation of Justice and the Vanishing Trial* paper, IALS WG Hart Legal Workshop 2006: The Retreat of the State: Challenges to Law and Lawyers.
[12] Menkel-Meadow, Carrie Is the Adversary System Really Dead? Dilemmas of Legal Ethics as legal Institutions and Roles Evolve (2004) 57 CLP 85 .
[13] Abel, Richard 'The Contradictions of Informal Justice' in *The Politics of Informal Justice* 1982 Academic Press, New York ed. Abel, R..
[14] The cost of England & Wales civil justice caused such concern that a judicial inquiry was set up under Lord Justice Jackson to investigate the matter, reporting in January, 2010.
[15] Galanter, Marc *The Privatisation of Justice and the Vanishing Trial* op. cit..

mediation industry has done little to increase public awareness of the distinction in an attempt to create its own mystique.

1.4 The Changing Role of the Lawyer

At its heart mediation is a form of intervention in which the lawyer – or more particularly the litigator or dispute resolution specialist - acts as gatekeeper of the dispute.

Mediation ideologies are reflective of the classification of various roles through which people intervene as third parties in the conflicts of others, not in the nature of the intervention but its degree.

Black & Baumgartner (1983)[16] identified a typology of twelve third parties offering partisan support roles ranging from **informer, adviser, advocate** and **ally** to **surrogate,** and non partisan roles involved in dispute processing as either a **facilitator** or having an arbitral function: from **friendly peacemaker, mediator, arbitrator** and **judge** to the **repressive peacemaker.** In therapeutic intervention the roles of **negotiator** and **healer** may be both partisan and non-partisan.

What is extraordinary is that a mediation advocate is likely during the various stages of his retainer, to play each of the twelve roles identified by this typology.

1.5 Lawyer or Non-Lawyer Advocate?

Under both the FCT and Lagos Rules, and more widely, all litigators must now have a basic understanding of the principles of mediation to be able to act in an advisory role. They not only have a responsibility to identify cases, both pre-and mid-proceedings, for which mediation is appropriate, and to explain the mediation process to clients and other legal professionals. They have specific tasks within the process –

---

[16] Black D. and Baumgartner M.P. 'Toward a Theory of the Third Party' in *Empirical Theories about Courts* 1983 Longman New York ed. Boyum K. and Mather L.

(1) Deciding to and persuading others to engage in the process

(2) Choosing the mediator

(3) Controlling the pre-mediation element

(4) Team leading at the mediation appointment

(5) Securing a working settlement

As advocates, they must be able to deal with all aspects of mediation within case management, something probably outside the remit or capability of non-lawyer mediation advocates. One such example concerns the enforceability of contractual mediation clauses. Most court schemes implicitly recognise a fairly formal facilitative model with a structured process, and consequently lawyer advocates will invariably use this model. However it is reasonable to suppose that mediators or neutrals who have been trained by the ABA or AMI, whether in Nigeria or in the United States, may have a more evaluative approach, which may be reflected where apposite in the powers granted to the Neutral in the mediation agreement.

PART 2

The Decision to Mediate

Chapter 2

THE DECISION TO MEDIATE

The Practice Directions of all members of the Network of Multi-Door Courthouses encourage parties to a dispute to use a 'walk-in' facility offered by each ADR Centre as a means of having an alternative to issuing process in litigation. Additionally the judges have embraced ADR by taking upon themselves the power of compulsion, signalled in *Jabita v. Onikoyi*[1] where the High Court of Lagos struck out both the main claim and counterclaim and directed the parties to ADR.[2]

Thus, as the lead mediation representative, occasionally the decision to mediate may be made for you, and you are presented with a mandatory contractual provision, a case management direction to that effect, or the prior agreement of the parties to the dispute before it arrives at your desk. More often than not you will be faced with making the decision yourself, either arising out of the curiosity of your lay client, a request from the other side or the court, or upon your own initiative. Don't wait to be asked. You should take the lead in a matter *so strategically and tactically important* in the context of the dispute whether it is already within or remains outside the formal adversarial process of litigation or arbitration. Statistically most disputes settle anyway before trial – a mediated settlement is likely to be any more or any less favourable, although it could be considerably more inventive - but settlement should occur much earlier, therefore with concomitant time and costs benefits.

To make the decision whether or not to have a case or dispute proceed to mediation requires:

- An understanding of the process: what mediation actually entails, and its different forms;

- An appreciation of possible outcomes to the dispute outside a negotiated agreement;

---

[1] [2004] All F.W.L.R. 1625
[2] See further at p.160-161.

- Sufficient knowledge of the strength of the legal case or of your client's then position;

- An understanding of the true value of the case to the client in terms of:

  (a) cost efficiency;

  (b) time efficiency;

  (c) what the client really wants to achieve if he can;

  (d) whether the remedy available from the court (even if achievable) can provide what is actually needed;

- Adequate knowledge of:

  (a) the client himself;

  (b) the client's wider business affairs;

  (c) any ongoing, or intended ongoing relationship between the parties – whether commercial, social or personal.

Without this information you will not be able to assess whether the decision *to permit the client to mediate* is correct. I lay stress on the words in italics. You are the advocate. You are charged with the responsibility for tactical decisions in managing the claim or its defence. It is not merely a question of applying mediation theory, or of being seduced by the ADR industry or even worrying unduly about costs sanctions in the litigation at this stage, although later this should become an important concern. You have to answer two basic questions:

1. Is the case suitable for mediation?

2. Is the case ripe for mediation?

The opening offer to mediate is still regarded in some quarters, mostly erroneously, as an indicator of weakness in a case that is being litigated. This stigma is based on the ignorance of the recipient, either of the process or the opportunity being presented, and such lack of knowledge takes time to eradicate. It does, however, lead to the second question and one that is of at least equal importance.

Mediation, yes (if the necessary parties can be persuaded), but if so, when? ADR may be utilised either before formal proceedings are issued or during the course of litigation or arbitration. To ascertain precisely when to call for ADR there are a number of questions you should consider.

Have you enough information about the claim, its defence, any cross-claim or third party entanglement?

Do the parties know and understand the issues being raised by each other?

Does each party at least know its own version of the facts?

Do you require full discovery, or have you sufficient to proceed?

Do you have a proper understanding of your own client's needs?

Are there non-parties to be brought in?

Is the timing tactically astute to apply pressure to your opponent by using the Rules, e.g. payment into court, to afford you the maximum protection for your client's position, and cause the other side maximum prejudice?

Conversely, is the potential cost saving such that mediation should be attempted as early as possible – even before proceedings have been issued?

Is it a dispute that will turn on expert or other technical evidence?

Is it possible to bring forward the time for ADR by obtaining early expert evidence or appointing a joint expert?

You really need to know the answer to each of these questions, not least to see if they are relevant to your client's situation.

Both of the key questions above should be placed in the context of meeting the client's best needs for resolving the dispute. That is why some distinguished commentators[3] and user organisations[4] now refer to 'ADR' not as '*alternative* dispute resolution', but rather as '*appropriate* dispute resolution.' The International Chamber of Commerce in Paris ADR Rules refer to the acronym as '*amicable* dispute resolution'.

As ADR processes become more sophisticated you must consider whether mediation is a better vehicle for settlement or determination of the issues

---

[3] For example Professor Jane Gordon, University of Oregon.
[4] Canadian National Energy Board; State of Oregon Department of Justice; United States Department of Education, Office of Special Education Programs National Centre on Dispute Resolution.

than early neutral assessment, or expert determination, or the executive mini-trial, or concilio-arbitration, or a traditional arbitration procedure. To do so you need to be familiar with the different strengths and weaknesses of these variations on mediation processes. You must have an awareness of the fact that a reference to ADR by the court does not mean mediation or bust.

2.1 Getting the Client to Mediate

The first essential is to introduce your client to and familiarise him with the concept of mediation. Most clients are extremely nervous of the court environment, but there is an inherent respect, sometimes a sense of awe, about our judicial process. The average client will be even less familiar with mediation and might worry about being rushed into a strange procedure. He may well need convincing that a non-arbitral process will suit his need, particularly since he is likely to regard the mediator as a form of judge, which, of course, he is not. Your client will certainly want reassurance that his legal representatives are familiar with and can be tactically astute while using this process.

Mediators are trained to investigate the potential for joint gains in resolving disputes. That is one of their most important tools in unlocking the potential for settlement. Be aware that this investigation applies equally to the advocate at every stage of the process, from persuading his own client, his solicitor or his opponent to agree to mediate, through to analysing and proposing constructive settlement opportunities on the day itself.

From the very outset you will have to consider both 'own client gains' and 'joint gains' as the means by which you can demonstrate to your client that mediation will suit his desired outcome. The most obvious examples are cost and time savings, certainty of outcome and control over the process. To persuade either your own client or both parties to mediate you will need to consider and identify what value there is in avoiding arguments over the merits of the case. Look outside the immediate remedies that the court can provide:

- Your client may have a strong case – either actual or perceived - but he may be unaware of: the value of his wasted time; his irrecoverable costs; the time of any witnesses, employees or co-workers both in preparing for litigation and attending court; the impact of such loss of time, whether in management or production, on a business or employment; the impact of publicity; and the cost, effectiveness and time for execution of a judgment or recovery under an order.

- Your client may have a weak case: he may not wish to test it in court, or you may advise that it should not be tested on the merits so as to avoid an adverse precedent being set.

- There may be collateral or parallel disputes outside the strict ambit of the present cause of action – further disputes that strictly fall outside any rule which may require that the parties should bring forward all matters between them in the same suit.

- There may be a further or ongoing relationship between the parties either not in dispute, or one that the parties cannot change. This may be commercial, social or economic. It may extend to family relationships, that of neighbours living in close proximity, or co-employees or those with a social connection who occupy shared work or leisure facilities or social amenities.

Advancing mediation as a practical solution presupposes that your client is considering settlement at all. If he is determined to have his day in court at any cost, that position may well change once the true costs of present day litigation start to mount up, and to bite. The Pre-Trial Conference or other case management may drive your client inevitably towards mediation, whether as a willing participant or not.

2.2 Dealing with the Client's Questions

You have to be prepared to advise your client why mediation is right for him in the particular circumstances of this case. You can show him the advantages and disadvantages. Be ready to deal with his reaction, in particular his questions, which will be a fairly conventional response from litigants unfamiliar with the process.

Questions generally fall into four categories: first he will think that he is being deprived of his day in court when the judge can say both to the parties and to the wider world that he was right. This is a matter to be dealt with in terms of litigation risk and cost/benefit analysis. In addition you can explain that he will be able to express his viewpoint personally, and seek vindication of his position, and that there may be considerable alternative 'own client gains.'

Directions given under the LMDC PD and AMDC PD will greatly assist the advocate in explaining both the policy of the ADR Judges and the element of compulsion to his or her client.

Second he does not want the approach to the other side to mediate to be seen as a sign of weakness. This should be dealt with by reference to the court rules on active case management, practice directions concerning mediation, a potential summons before the ADR Judge, the impact of declining to participate in ADR on the overall discretion of the court to award costs, and the fact that any initial approach could be made by the MD Court itself, or a private mediation service provider rather than you or your firm or solicitor.

Third, your client may ask how much the process of mediation will cost. His concern is that this represents a waste of money if no settlement is achieved. You will be able to explain the statistical success rate, and the fact that the mediation process creates a momentum towards settlement, even if no agreement is concluded on the day. You will ask him to consider the collateral benefits the mediation may bring within the litigation by reducing or clarifying issues, and enabling both you and him to have a good look at how the other side are likely to shape up at trial.

Finally he will want to know who is the right mediator or neutral. If he gets to that stage, he is already engaging in the process. At an early juncture you will either have a mediation service provider in mind, or if you are experienced in a particular field or have represented parties in successful mediations before, a list of appropriate individual mediators.

2.3 Key Points to Explain

The client needs to be able to make an informed choice. Any explanation you give is likely to have regard to the following points:

(i) Your client's understanding of the role of the mediator is likely to be wrong. This process is not the imposition of a decision by a third party, but a consensual attempt to solve the problem in hand, and, where possible, any collateral or wider issues between the parties that exist or can be foreseen. Your client may be looking for goals to be achieved beyond the ambit of the existing dispute. Be that as it may, you must be able to rationalise the need for a mediator rather than have an *inter-partes* negotiation. The mediator will be a confidential listener and a shuttle diplomat; he will filter parties communications with each other, absorb any emotional antagonism and push the parties to focus on underlying objectives rather than posturing or staking out a position; he will encourage joint problem solving, suggest appropriate compromises, offer non-binding views on the merits (if pressed to do so) and also ask tough questions to discover and mirror to them the strengths and weaknesses of a party's case.[5]

(ii) The legal framework exists under the substantive law of the relevant states (e.g the LMDC Law, the FCT Rules, the Kano MDC Bill etc.) to protect your client's position; in particular it operates as a safety net. You will need to place emphasis on the "without prejudice" nature of the proceedings, the fact that they are confidential and that information exchanged or obtained in the course of a mediation may not be used elsewhere[6] afterwards, including in the litigation.

(iii) The ability or extent to which the process is consensual: your client may leave the mediation at any point, for example under the LMDC PD or AMDC PD.

(iv) The fact that the mediation proposed may come under the ambit of a particular local court-annexed scheme if the dispute is contained within a certain jurisdiction. If that is the case there may be an element of compulsion, particularly if voluntary take up under the scheme is low.

(v) Once a settlement has been agreed, it becomes enforceable as a matter of contract, and as long as it is workable the courts will enforce it.[7] Under s.19 LMDC Law and Article 17 LMDC PD; Ord r4(3) High Court of Lagos (Civil Procedure) Rules 2004; and s.11 Sheriff and Civil Process Law, once reduced to writing and signed by the parties a settlement agreement is forwarded for endorsement to the Referral Judge (court-referred matters) or the ADR Judge (walk-in and Direct Intervention matters) and deemed to be enforceable as a judgment of the High Court of Lagos.

For commercial clients it should be stressed that Nigeria has produced over the last few years a number of well qualified, easily available and fairly priced mediators, including specialist practitioners.

In addition foreign mediators may be used privately where this is seen as costs effective, called on from the UK, Canada, America and South Africa. Most mediators entirely undervalue the gift they bring to clients. Although

---

[5] Mackie, Karl *The Effective Mediator* CEDR seminar paper February 2002.
[6] *Venture Investment Placement Ltd v Hall* [2005] EWHC 1227 (Ch) and *Reed Executive Plc v Reed Business Information* [2004] EWCA Civ 887; [2004] 1 WLR 3026 applying *Rush & Tompkins Ltd v GLC* [1989] AC 1290 HL. But cf Part 6
[7] Foskett QC, David *The Law and Practice of Compromise* 6th edn 2005 Thomson Sweet & Maxwell ch.10,11 and 43.

their functions are very different, you can make the point that a mediator can be chosen, unlike a judge.

Large corporate clients often present a problem at this stage, and sometimes later in the process. In a multi-layered or institutional concern, whether in the private or public sector, the question to mediate has to be placed before the appropriate decision-maker by his internal advisers. In organisations where there may be a blame culture there is a risk that people would rather not make a decision than make one and get it wrong. You may have to overcome this kind of culture and stand firm in advising that mediation should be tried, and at what stage in the management of the dispute.

Be sympathetic to a reluctant client. In many cases it is a hard decision for him to make not to fight a case in which he has belief, and he may be concerned reasonably about the 'blink first' mentality or what he perceives as an additional layer of costs. These perceptions can be overcome by demonstrating that entry into a mediation is relatively risk-free: in a process which is non-adjudicative and non-binding you have the flexibility to act outside the constraints of the relevant High Court Rules and to exploit the dynamics of mediation procedure to the best advantage of your client. The court will give you credit for having engaged in the process even if it does not succeed. If it fails, although the costs may have been wasted, costs which are outside the scope of the mediation agreement itself will generally become costs in the case.[8] Unlike the strictures of litigation advocacy you have the opportunity to devise solutions to the problem, rather than present evidence and argument in an attempt to prove your client's position, and to address what the other side is saying, rather than score points from your opponent.

2.4 Getting Your Instructing Solicitor or Principal to Agree to Mediation

It should follow from what we have said thus far that mediation is not an arena for the unskilled or the naïve. However, the barrier to engaging in this process may not come from the lay client: there may be resistance from your instructing solicitor, if you are counsel, or from your principal should you have one. Opposition may be due to the same problems of perception that accords with the initial reaction of the lay client. Although most major firms now embrace all forms of dispute resolution as part of their litigation departments,

---

[8] See Part 7.3.

there is still a fairly widespread and genuine lack of enlightenment among senior lawyers, a prejudice to the effect that this process is somehow less lawyerly, and a worry about lowering of fee income in contentious business. For many 'ADR' is seen as *'Alarming Drop in Revenue.'* They haven't the foresight to recognise the marketing power of the truly satisfied client.

You will need to argue that where mediation is entirely suited to the client's particular needs, and the court will, in applying active case management, regard it as suitable for the particular claim, your instructing solicitor or principal should take the credit for promoting it to the client. If the mediation is successful, even though there might be a diminution in the fee income that could otherwise have been achieved by litigating the particular case to trial, the firm will have achieved client satisfaction, leading to a strengthened relationship. The litigation may well have settled anyway - considerably over 90% of issued claim forms never get to trial. And if the mediation fails, the fee income is still available.

See whether there is or will be an impasse in any negotiations towards settlement; whether factors exist which suggest a compromise of the claim will be difficult, for example a serious power or economic imbalance between the parties, or a link between this dispute and other disputes (or present litigation). You may advise your instructing solicitor or principal that rather than pursue fruitless negotiations which may take months to lead nowhere, he should take the credit in the eyes of the court for moving the process along by proposing mediation.

At an early stage in the dispute you will be able to see if there is either a contractual trigger into mediation, or a court procedural directive – whether a local or jurisdictional-based court annexed or referred scheme, or an ad-hoc industry based process.

2.5 Getting The Other Side to Agree to Mediation

Despite its many advantages mediation is not a panacea, and there are cases where it is not appropriate; as I have stressed, timing is equally, if not more important. Therefore as a pre-cursor I can not stress highly enough that you should not propose mediation to the other side unless and until you are satisfied that:

- it is appropriate for the dispute;
- your client understands what it is and why he should agree to it;

- it is the right tactic; and
- the time is right.[9]

The second obstacle you need to consider is the opposing party's expectation of the strength of its case and the likely outcome of a trial. Whatever view you take of the strength or otherwise of your own client's position you need to recognise that there may be serious and good faith differences between the parties' forecasts of the likely result. This operates to create a settlement gap that is difficult to bridge.

Thirdly, where relevant you should ponder the complexity of any situation in which you are instructed in a multi-party, multi-issue dispute. In most cases this should encourage mediation, but occasionally it can be a hurdle, and is likely to be perceived as such by any other party that is unfamiliar with mediation techniques for multi-party claims.

(1)   If the subject matter of the dispute is contractual first see if there is an ADR/mediation clause, and, if so, whether it is mandatory and enforceable.[10] Whether mandatory or not, the existence of the clause should be drawn to the attention of the other side at the earliest opportunity. Let your opponent have the burden of explaining to a court why it should not be utilised.

(2)   See if the other side's lawyers or professional advisors are members of NCMG, SPIDR, AFMA, SCMA or CEDR or one of the other widely recognised mediation service providers. Suggest that their opposition to mediation in your case is inconsistent with their membership of organisations promoting mediation.

(3)   Point out that Ord. 25 r.2(c) Lagos Rules or Ord. 17(a) FCT Rules and the professional duty of lawyers both as officers of the court and under the obligation they owe to do best for their client require consideration of ADR anyway. Courts are serious about using the process. Therefore where appropriate invite them to consider the practice directions provided for.

(4)   If the other side have no prior experience of mediation and need an independent explanation of the process, provide it with some

---

[9] See Dodson, Charles *Preparing for Mediation* (1997) 17 Resolutions, CEDR.
[10] See e.g. *R G Carter Ltd v Edmund Nuttall Ltd* (2002) BLR 59; *O'Callaghan v Coral Racing Ltd* [1998] EWCA Civ 1801; *N v N* [1999] Fam. Div LTL Lawtel AC7800507.

educational material from any MDC.

(5)   Show that the relevant business/social relationship can be preserved/resumed.

(6)   Underline that it is non-binding and therefore has little downside.

(7)   Where appropriate show that it is obvious that a creative commercial solution that the court cannot provide is the most desirable outcome for the parties.

(8)   Reiterate that although mediation is no longer cheap in absolute terms, it remains a cheaper option than litigation taken to trial. High Court fees alone are considerably more expensive than those of the MDCs.

(9)   A close analysis of the UK case of *Halsey*[28] suggests that judges will consider imposing costs sanctions on parties who decline mediation whether a judge recommends it or otherwise. In Nigeria State High Courts have the power to strike out claims altogether for such failure.

(10)   For opponents who purport genuinely not to know the advantages of mediation they are these:

    • It is desirable to be able to control the outcome of the dispute rather than have it imposed upon you, potentially leaving both parties dissatisfied by the experience. Many 'winners' find that in real terms, taking into account time, irrecoverable costs and aggravation, they have not won anything at all.

    • Where each side has some merit this may be reflected in a fairer outcome than the court is able to provide.

    • The absence of a trial not necessarily wanted by both parties has its advantages: reduced costs, no full trial preparation, the litigation is not so protracted, and the absence of findings of fact that might subsequently be used by one of the parties.

    • Generally there is a very speedy resolution.

- Those interests which are of real importance to either or both parties will not be obscured by technical or legal issues advanced by the lawyers within the framework of the litigation.

- There may be no real point in trying to fight against a legal principle where the determinative legal issues are already well settled.

- There may be a need to avoid an adverse precedent, and this consideration may attach itself to both sides.

- One or both parties may have good reasons to avoid the publicity which, potentially at least, is always thrown up by litigation whether at a local or even national level.

- One or both parties desires that, for commercial or other reasons, the existence of the dispute itself should not become known.

- One or both parties may have a desire to limit the discovery they would otherwise have to provide in the course of the action.

- A party has discovery which would be embarrassing, either in the context of the dispute, or generally.

- A party has trade or business secrets which it would prefer not to reveal but which might become public if the case went to trial.

- The case may settle before trial, and if so it is as well to try and stop it sooner rather than later. There may be no good reason why the case should not settle, but it requires the impetus of objective and outside thought.

- Perhaps neither side really wants to litigate, even though there are commercial or social reasons for doing so.

- A mediator will help diffuse the emotion or hostility that may otherwise bar any settlement.

- The uncertain outcome of a trial is generally a good reason to mediate.

If you cannot persuade your opponent to consider mediation, or if, for some good reason, you feel uncomfortable in doing so, one of the functions of a mediation service provider is to approach the other side at an early juncture to explore the desirability of mediation. Use an experienced neutral third party or a mediation service provider to break down the resistance to mediate. They will be better practised than you in dealing with the range of excuses made to evade the process because of its unsuitability for this case. They will be able to answer the typical assertions that mediation is not appropriate because the case is too complex, there are different legal opinions on the merits, the experts cannot agree, or there is too much or too little at stake. In the UK current judicial thought after *Halsey* is that there is only a limited range of cases where mediation is in fact unsuitable – the desire for a public law precedent, a clear case for summary judgment, and where urgent injunctive relief is required. Even in the latter a claim can certainly proceed to mediation after an interim order is made.

The MDC court-annexed schemes should by now have overcome the 'don't blink first' mentality of litigants and their lawyers, and also ironed out any stance where a party insists on pre-conditions before entering the process. The strong support shown by the court for confidentiality,[11] affording the contents of the mediation the same status as "without prejudice" negotiations, is designed to give confidence to the parties.

2.6 Arguing Against Mediation

As an advocate you must know equally how to argue against your client being pushed into a mediation that you consider inappropriate to meet his or her needs.

While the combined effect of the FCT Rules and LMDC and AMDC PD is that all members of the legal profession who conduct litigation should now routinely consider with their clients whether their dispute is suitable for ADR, that most cases are to be regarded as suitable for mediation, and that (short of compulsion) a judge's encouragement for parties to go to ADR may be robust and he will not necessarily accept an unwillingness at face value,

---

[11] *Venture Investment Placement Ltd v Hall* [2005] EWHC 1227 (Ch) and *Reed Executive Plc v Reed Business Information* [2004] EWCA Civ 887; see also Part 6.

you have to be able to withstand such pressure if you genuinely believe it is wrong for your client on the facts as you know them to be.

We have touched upon the factors which will impede the court's charge towards mediation above. These concern situations where:

(a)   At least one side requires a precedent.[12]

(b)   There is in fact (or law) no bona fide dispute - one side's position is devoid of merit.

(c)   Your client needs a remedy which mediation cannot achieve, namely an injunction or other mandatory or prohibitory order of the court.

There are other arguments available to resist the drive towards mediation, or tactical considerations by reason of which your client should not engage the mediation process at this particular stage in the action. For example:

(a)   The advantage of delay heavily favours one side.

(b)   The case can be settled soon through unassisted negotiations.

(c)   Conversely, there is no motivation to settle at all.

(d)   One party requires a full open court personal vindication.

(e)   The case concerns criminal activity, family relationships or requires the paramountcy of the court's jurisdiction.

(f)   There are vital corporate interests involved.

(g)   The amount in dispute is extremely large.

(h)   Taken together with any of the previous factors, more time is needed to properly evaluate each side's position and settlement possibilities.[13]

(i)   In the context of the foregoing matter, expert evidence is needed before the decision to mediate can be taken.

---

[12] *McCook v Lobo* [2002] EWCA Civ 1760.
[13] *SITA v Wyatt* [2002] EWHC 2401 Ch; *Corenso v Burnden* [2003] EWHC 1805 (QB).

(j)   There has not been sufficient discovery.

(k)   In the particular circumstances of the case there should be an exchange of witness statements first.

(l)   Where on any view the cost/benefit analysis suggests that the costs of the mediation will be disproportionate to the value of the claim.

Approach your argument against having a mediation with care and particularity. If the case proceeds to trial even if you win the court may wish to consider whether ADR was unreasonably refused, and will look at all of the pertinent circumstances including the nature of the dispute, the merits of the case, whether other settlement methods had been attempted, whether the costs of ADR might have been disproportionately high, whether the delay to accommodate some form of mediation would have delayed the trial significantly, and whether ADR had a reasonable prospect of success. Your or your client's belief in the strength of the case is not of itself a ground for refusing mediation, and a judge may well deprive a winning party of his costs if he concludes that mediation would have been suitable, was likely to be fruitful and should at least have been tried.

Part 3

Choosing a Mediator

Chapter 3

CHOOSING A MEDIATOR

Each MDC ADR Centre has slightly different rules for the appointment of a mediator, but broadly speaking each institution maintains a panel of qualified and experienced Neutrals who have been trained to the requisite standard of competency, and who will comply with local codes of practice and ethics in respect of their role and conduct. From such panels of Neutrals the parties are usually provided with a short list of relevant candidates and then encouraged to agree a suitable Neutral to act as mediator according to his or her content area, expertise and the dynamics of the case. In some instances the MDC or administrative Dispute Resolution Officer ('DRO') will offer an appointment of one individual, but this must be subject to the approval of the parties.

For an advocate the ability to choose the composition of your tribunal is an unusual and illuminating experience. Although it cannot be stressed too highly that a mediator has no arbitral powers and is not going to be a decision maker, the parties will undoubtedly respect him or her as a figure of authority as the chairman and convenor of the proceedings, and will rely upon his gravitas and experience. He will in fact assist in adjudicating on procedural matters, usually by providing direction and making positive suggestions with which the parties are expected to agree. Invariably your lay client is likely to regard him as a sort of judge, even though you must make it plain that he is not.

As an advocate, more often than not you may only be instructed after the mediator has been appointed. However, when available, the opportunity to select the appropriate mediator should never be wasted. Guidance over the selection is no less a function of the advocate than any other pre-hearing advisory work, and should be approached with care. If you are asked to advise at an early stage in the dispute there are two important practical questions to consider in choosing a mediator. Firstly, in respect of disputes outside the remit of the Court or an MDC, and prior to litigation commencing, should a private sector mediation service provider be appointed? Secondly, and should the mediator himself or herself be a lawyer, do you require an expert in the area of the dispute, or else an experienced layman (i.e. non-lawyer)?

You are looking for a mediator who has a number of qualities. Apart from having obtained an appropriate qualification from, and continuing professional education or current accreditation with, a recognised mediation training body, you need a person of reasonable experience having some knowledge of, if not expertise in, the area of the dispute. He or she needs to have a good bedside manner, with the common touch – hand holding is an integral part of the mediator's skill, since he also requires patience, and the ability to absorb a party's frustration, anger or anxiety. You will want as a candidate someone with innovative ideas or problem-solving skills who is a good communicator, and exudes a sense of authority without pomposity. He will himself need to be an advocate in the sense of being proficient in examining and testing a party's stated position and to deal readily with the consequences.

3.1 Choosing the Right Mediator

Whether you opt for a mediation service provider or not, you still have to decide or agree who is the right mediator for your client. Presupposing that those institutions who train mediators provide accreditation and continuing education to a set quality threshold, and that the procedures, method and practice in which each train their own particular mediators are broadly similar, the question for you is how to match the most appropriate and desirable mediator to your dispute.

First, since you are an advocate, consider whether you want a mediator who is also a lawyer by professional background, if not actually in practice. The advantages are readily apparent: experienced litigators and counsel develop well-honed practical skills in critical analysis, problem solving and communication. They can be incisive in identifying key issues and focussing upon the factual and legal merits of a particular position. A mediator who is familiar with the area of law in question can, if called upon to do so, engage in debate on the law, know the key cases and recognise the legal merits of the parties' respective positions. A lawyer may also have practical experience of litigating disputes of the type being mediated.

Specialist lawyer mediators will readily understand the legal and commercial context in which the dispute sits; they will gain the respect of both advocates and their lay clients more quickly; there need be no time wasted in laboured explanation; the lay parties' suspicion, wariness or frustration may thus be minimised. They will be aware of procedural timetabling, case management and the impact of costs in the litigation.

Having said that, whilst you and your opposite number may be conscious of the legal parameters and merits of the dispute, a non-lawyer mediator may have a completely different overview of the settlement objectives of the parties. He is far less likely to be concerned about legal practicalities or niceties, and will be less interested in whether or not you will be able to prove your case to a court on another occasion. In that sense a non-lawyer mediator may be of greater appeal to a party that has an obviously weaker case in law.

You should be aware that a non-lawyer mediator will not welcome being tied down to arguments concerning the legal aspects of the dispute. He may make you feel undue haste in getting to the horse-trading part of the process. He may be keener than a lawyer mediator to separate you from your client in the sense that he will regard you as the gatekeeper of your client's legal interests – he will not be terribly concerned about those legal interests – since his objective is to find a solution to the dispute using means that may well fall substantially outside of the legal constraints and procedures that you associate with the litigation. If such a mediator makes you feel uncomfortable please remember he is not a judge, and neither his task nor the process itself is intended to impose a settlement on your client.

Both advocates and lawyer mediators need to guard against a strictly legal analysis of the dispute. This may be difficult for all lawyers. The importance of analysing a dispute in the broadest terms and not confining it to its strictly legal nature is underlined by the approach of mediation training organisations when teaching new mediators to distinguish between facilitative and evaluative mediation. Evaluative mediation is essentially opinion forming, and lawyer mediators have great difficulty in refraining from making value judgments about the parties' positions. At least they can learn to restrain themselves from expressing an opinion unless expressly called upon to do so.

With a plethora of mediators now available the expertise and experience of your potential candidate is of real importance. You have the ability to select for your hearing a mediator who is an acknowledged authority in his specialist field, be it medical, technical, financial or legal. He will be able to identify most known solutions to common problems in that area and, hopefully, adapt them to fit the parties' particular circumstances.

In certain circumstances you may consider that a non-lawyer, non-specialist mediator happens to be the right person, particularly if he comes by recommendation to you or your party. Both you and your client need to feel confident that he will observe confidentiality; that he will exercise control over the proceedings, and certainly that he is able to control time; that he will keep all parties informed of what is going on; that he is seen to be neutral; that he has sufficient gravitas and authority – a particular advantage of using a former judge; that he has no personal agenda, is not a bully, will be even-handed, patient and an innovative problem solver, whether evaluative or facilitative.[1]

You may have to advise whether or not co-mediators are required. If there are a large number of parties or issues a single mediator may not be able to have sufficient creativity, or indeed time: mediator teams are useful in working with parties to build up trust and dealing with cultural or jurisdictional differences. A mediation team can be mixed between a lawyer and an expert, or mediators from or experienced in the separate cultures or jurisdictions. The appointment of a mediation team means that more than one activity can take place simultaneously at the hearing. Where a mediation team is involved, one solution that is sometimes adopted is to re-constitute as a form of arbitral hearing involving findings by a number of the mediation team who has not previously engaged in any confidential discussions. Whether or not a mediation team adopts such a solution, it is crucial that the members have complementary skills and work well together.

In the article *'Choose Carefully: All Mediators Are Not Created Equal'* from his series *Mediation Strategies*[2] the well-known California mediator, Lee Jay Berman, advises if a mediation is going to have a chance at success, perhaps the most important decision is who will sit in the neutral chair at the head of the table. From case to case, that decision will vary. Advocates owe it to their clients to invest the time in investigating, strategising and selecting the right mediator for each case. He suggests that in a time when we have retired judges, litigators, transactional advocates, and professional mediators available, and when more mediators are specialising in particular areas of practice, the best way to select the right mediator requires a strategy.

He recommends, among others, the following considerations

- mediators need to be selected on a consensus basis, rather than a least objectionable or lowest-common-denominator basis. Mediation

---

[1] The European Code of Conduct for Mediators has specific provisions about impartiality and confidentiality.
[2] See www.mediate.com archive material and the SCMA website newsletter archive at www.mediationadvocates.org.uk

has a greater chance of settling the case if all parties believe in the mediator's reputation, personality and qualifications.

• Just because the other side has proposed a mediator that they have worked with before, that is no reason to object to that mediator. The mediator has no ability to make you agree to anything you don't want to, nor can they coerce or pressure you or your client. If the other advocate is proposing a mediator they are probably doing so because they feel that mediator at least can be trusted and has a client rapport, or has the ability to settle the case, which means finding mutually agreeable terms for settlement.

• Consider the level of actual mediation training your mediator has. After all, if settling the case was easy to do, you wouldn't need a third party to assist you and your opposing number.

• Consider the mediator's record for tenacity to see the case through to resolution. A mediator can only keep going if they have the skills to keep trying different things, and if they have what some have called "an iron rear end" and are willing to sit and keep working for as long as it takes to get a case resolved. That tenacity, or resolve to settle a case, is one of the most important features to look for in evaluating a mediator, and in interviewing other counsel who have worked with that mediator in the past.

• Ask your opposite number about the type of mediator to which they would best respond. Some cases (and sometimes your opposite number) require an authoritative voice of a retired judge or litigator with decades of experience. Others may respond better to a persuasive, personable mediator who reaches people well and can see the big picture. Some cases require a macho authority figure, while others may do better with a more sensitive touch. It is important to consider variables such as these in each case. No case will be like any other, since the personalities at the table will be different and will respond to different types of mediators. You will also need to consider your relationship with your opposite number and whether you want your mediator to provide more of a facilitated negotiation or an evaluative appraisal of the case.

• Consider your client's state of mind. If they are highly emotional about the case, they will benefit (as will you) from a mediator who can handle emotional parties and help move them to a place where they can make a decision, gently guiding the case to a smooth settlement. If they are stubborn and intransigent, they may need logic and tenacious persuading. If they are weak decision-makers or are unsure about the fair value of their case, they may need the authority of a retired judge or seasoned litigator.

- Consider your own strengths and weaknesses. This may be the hardest part, but it is critical to know yourself with clarity. For example, if you have a strong, authoritative presence, you may benefit from a mediator who has a softer touch to complement you. If you tend to be more left-brained, or a more logical or linear thinker, you may want a mediator who is more right-brained, more emotionally attuned, and perhaps creative. If you have a client control problem, you may want a mediator whose style is more firm and directive.

- Consider the timing of the case. If your case is directed towards mediation by a date that you believe is too early in the case, and you are unable to persuade the judge of this, then you will want to select a tenacious mediator who is dedicated to following the case through the litigation process. Experienced mediators know that sometimes, the early mediation appointment is only the start of the mediation process, and that additional key disclosure may be required before a final settlement can be reached. You will want a mediator who is a real believer in peaceful resolutions and in not letting litigation get out of control unnecessarily. This could range from a no-nonsense retired judge to a former general counsel to a non-advocate mediator with business and economic sense.

- Consider the subject matter. It is not imperative, but it is helpful to have a mediator who understands the nature of the dispute. If the dispute is dissolution of a family business, it can be helpful to have a mediator who understands partnership, business and contract law. It could also be beneficial to have a mediator who is familiar with the workings of the particular industry in which the family operates their business. It may be even more beneficial to have a mediator who specialises in, or understands the unique dynamics of family businesses. The important thing to consider in selecting the mediator is that they are familiar with what it takes to discuss the issues and to reach a resolution. It is not enough for the mediator to understand the legal issues; he or she must understand how to relate enough to the parties and their legal team to bring the parties to a mutually agreeable resolution.

- Consider the difficulty level of the case. Many smaller cases can be less complex, such as a simple debt collection or personal injury case that most mediators might be able to resolve. Other cases are the type that only a small percentage of mediators can settle. For example, a wrongful death case may include legal issues, insurance coverage issues, medical issues, deep emotional loss issues, and structured settlement issues, and will require a very experienced mediator with lots of tools and skills. You will benefit by trying to match the skill level of the mediator to the difficulty level of the case. Some advocates will look at a very difficult case and assume that any mediation will fail, so they will pay little attention to the selection of mediator. Instead, try hiring a highly skilled mediator and give the mediation process a chance to settle the case.

- Ask colleagues for useful information as outlined above. Ask specific questions about each of these points, rather than simply asking if your colleague liked the mediator or thought he or she was competent. Even less informative is asking whether the case settled, since there are so many variables involved in whether a case settles or not, this may be the worst indicator of the mediator's skill and effectiveness.

As Berman says, the selection of your mediator may be the most important decision you make regarding the mediation. Take the time to read through c.v.s, ask colleagues, and do the appropriate research, taking responsibility for making it succeed. After all, there are few experiences more frustrating than putting several hours of hard work into a mediation, only to have it fail. Make the decision wisely.

3.2 Mediation Service Providers

If litigation has not yet commenced the great advantage of using a private sector mediation service provider is the provision of administrative support, and a package which, for a global fee paid equally by both parties, will usually consist of:

- the supply of a recommended mediator on an approved list or accredited panel,

- his or her preparation and attendance,

- locating and hiring as necessary the venue,

- the management of the process from agreement to mediate until its conclusion.

Management of the process normally includes:

(i)   providing explanatory material on the process itself;

(ii)   identifying a shortlist of approved or accredited mediators experienced in such disputes, together with c.v. or résumé for each;

(iii)   supplying an up to date standard form mediation agreement into which the parties will enter, together with the mediator;

(iv)   agreeing and settling the mediator's instructions and remuneration;

(v)   booking and dealing with the owners of the venue;

(vi)   meeting any queries or problems raised by the parties, or the mediator;

(vii)   co-ordinating the arrangements with the parties' lawyers;

(viii)   conducting any post-mediation procedures.

There are now dozens of mediation service providers, ranging from training organisations, academic or professional institutions and trade bodies to private commercial firms. Absent using such a service most experienced mediators can be contacted directly.

You should choose a service provider with a substantial panel of mediators whose recommendations you can trust. You are looking for an organisation that will identify the right mediator for your dispute, and not merely nominate the same few, albeit highly experienced mediators, irrespective of the subject matter of the dispute, who are their trainers or faculty members. Its panel should have broad areas of expertise, and it must provide a fully administered service. This avoids contact directly with the mediator over minor but important details, which is likely to increase costs.

A fully administered service will:

   •   Help the parties agree the appropriate resolution process to use;

   •   Encourage reluctant parties to engage in the process;

   •   Advise on the appropriate mediator or neutral, or, where necessary and appropriate, the team of neutrals;

- Undertake and obtain a conflict check from the neutral;

- Provide as necessary a declaration of the neutral's independence;

- Negotiate the neutral's fee on behalf of parties and deal with his or her remuneration;

- Advise on the contents of the documents bundle;

- Advise on the contents of the case summaries;

- Seek to achieve a numerical balance between the parties attending the hearing;

- Secure from each party an agreement to the terms of the mediation or provide a standard form agreement for adoption, or as the basis for further discussion and amendment to suit the particular dispute;

- Secure and organise the venue, dealing with any problems that may arise;

- Provide the mediator with engrossed copies of the mediation agreement for signature by the parties on the day of the hearing;

- Deliver the appropriate papers to the mediator;

- Generally ensure that the process goes smoothly.

When selecting a service provider you should check precisely what the fee will include, and that the service provides all of the preceding matters.[3]

---

[3] Fees may be negotiable.

PART 4

The Pre-Mediation Process

Chapter 4

THE PRE-MEDIATION PROCESS

4.1 Choosing the Venue

The Multi-Door Courthouses and ADR Centres in Lagos, FCT Abuja, Kano, Abia, Akwa Ibom and Kaduna, and the Department of People's Rights in the Ministry of Justice of Delta State each envisage that court-annexed mediation appointments will take place in the precincts of those courts and centres. In addition there will be an open private sector which offers accommodation for mediations.

Outside those fixed court sites, depending upon their jurisdiction, you will have the opportunity to consider the most appropriate location for the mediation appointment, and should do so in geographical, physical, strategic and tactical terms.

First discover whether the cost of the venue is included in any global fee. This should be the case if a mediation service provider is being used, otherwise there may be a separate hire charge raised. If an additional cost is being incurred consider whether it may be preferable to have the mediation cost free at the offices or chambers of one of the parties or their legal team. Identify where your clients, any attendees coming on their behalf, the other side and the mediator are located and propose the most central location where facilities are available. Mediators consider that reaching agreement on matters such as the venue and format of the mediation session is an important psychological step towards settlement; at least it moves the parties from areas of disagreement towards areas of agreement prior to the meeting.

In a two-party mediation a minimum of three rooms are usually required, one large enough for all participants, and two for private sessions. Where there are only two meeting rooms, one party will have private sessions in the plenary room. If there are insufficient rooms for the numbers attending, parties may have to make do with corridors, which is unsatisfactory. If the availability of rooms is generous the mediator may take the opportunity of having small parallel or simultaneous meetings between, for example, the experts, or the lawyers, while he pursues settlement avenues elsewhere. Whoever or whatever organisation hosts the mediation session, refreshments will have to be provided during the day and made available should the session go into the evening. The rooms should be accessible, comfortable, lit with natural light and heated, since parties may be occupying them for lengthy periods. The parties' rooms need to have outside telephone lines, and the host should make available wi-fi or broadband, fax and photocopying facilities, the first three to obtain additional information or documents, and the last to ensure that any agreement is copied and distributed to all parties and the mediator prior to leaving the building, and afterwards to the mediation service provider. If at all possible, the venue needs to be staffed into the night, and information should be made available to the parties concerning local transport including taxis, last train times, parking availability after business hours, and local restaurants or takeaway services.

Strategic and tactical considerations often revolve around the question "where should the mediation take place: at our side's, their side's or a neutral venue?" Occasionally parties to a dispute, particularly defendant's solicitors or insurers believe that there is a tactical advantage in having control of the venue and requiring the claimant to attend their premises. If this is seen as a form of intimidation it will hardly be conducive to settlement. If having the mediation at one party's premises is genuinely, or can be portrayed as, a convenient cost-saving device, that is more acceptable. Invariably the mediator will prefer the parties to meet at a neutral location. For you the most important thing is that your client should feel comfortable and believe that the location, as in all other things, is a demonstration of the even-handedness of the process. He should not be put under pressure to accept a situation he does not want, nor feel he is being inconvenienced either by the other side or the mediator.

4.2 The Mediation Agreement

The legal basis for mediation is contractual. Even the LMDC and AMDC Practice Directions which enable the respective High Courts to direct parties into mediation require[1] that the parties, the mediator and the LMDC/AMDC will enter into a mediation agreement in relation to the confidentiality and conduct of the process.

Despite the fact that MDCs, mediation service providers, or indeed mediators working independently, will provide the parties with a current standard form mediation agreement which they have devised, a lawyer or

---

[1] See Article 5.

party representative should review and, if necessary, revise the mediation documentation with input from the client. It may well be that someone with far more mediation experience than you has settled the agreement, but those appearing in mediation must take their clients through the document so that its terms are both comprehensive to the dispute and fully understood.

There are certain key points which must be found in every mediation agreement:

(i)   The entire proceedings are confidential and without prejudice to the extent the law permits.

(ii)   No party may call the mediator to give evidence in later proceedings of what he has learned in the course of the mediation.[2] This prohibition extends to costs proceedings.

(iii)   The process is voluntary (including within the framework of the MDC Practice Directions): any party can call a halt to the proceedings without sanction.

(iv)   The mediator's role is to facilitate a settlement, not to pass any judgment or make any findings.

(v)   The terms of any agreed settlement are to be in writing.

In addition to these fundamental provisions, it is possible to agree the format or contents of the mediation by the insertion of agreed protocols into the agreement. Examples of such usual clauses as these are:

The parties will have authority to settle on the day.

The parties will observe the mediator's directions.

The parties will remain at the mediation for a minimum of one private session each.

---

[2] The question of the compellability of a mediator was one of the central features of *Farm Assist Ltd v DEFRA (No.2)* [2009] EWHC 1102 TCC in which the court concluded that a separate 'mediation privilege' was vested in the mediator, but that this could be overridden in certain circumstances. See Part 6 for a further discussion. As a consequence the wording of the Mediation Agreement should extend the mediator's privilege beyond the pre-existing dispute to cover the entirety of the mediation process, including post-mediation appointment work of any kind performed by him or her, and any settlement agreement.

The mediation may be terminated in the event of a specified circumstance.

The parties will not record/tape the mediation sessions.

Some standard form mediation agreements now extend to fairly sizeable documents with explanatory notes and guidance as to the conduct of the mediator. Good examples of two of these are to be found at Appendix 1.[3]

4.3 Document Preparation

It may be a broad generalisation but documents rarely play an important part in mediation, and the production of bundles comparable to a trial is certainly unnecessary on most occasions. That is because you are not trying to prove your case, although it may be vital to your negotiating stance that the mediator and the other side are made aware of how you see the strength of your position which, presumably, you will be able to support with objective documentary evidence. The strength of the legal case is ever-present as a frame of reference (see Fig. 1: 'the Box' at p.16 above). Bundles should be minimal however, perhaps the equivalent of a jointly agreed core bundle comprising only key documents and, if the dispute is in litigation, the salient court documents.

Remember that the mediator will need sufficient material to 'hit the ground running' since he is being asked to guide the parties in only a few hours to the resolution of a dispute which is likely to have been running for months if not years. He will need such time as you consider necessary for him to absorb the facts and key arguments, undertake some background research and consider possible strategies in advance of commencing the negotiation.

Having said that, the typical fee for the mediator will only allow for a relatively short period of preparation, unless additional reading time is specifically agreed beforehand, or the mediator is paid a separate hourly fee. Bear in mind what the role of the mediator is going to be. There is no point in running up a bill for preparing bundles of documents that the mediator will not use.

For the advocate the task of identifying minimum key documents becomes very important. You will need to focus on those items vital to establish the background – limiting the statements of case or other case management material to only those needed to understand the issues - and those

---

[3] See pp. 175-189.

necessary for you to establish your case or undermine that of your opponent. All non-essential documents should be rejected. This means that *inter-partes* correspondence is seldom to be included unless you consider it absolutely crucial.[4]

The primary purpose of the documents is not to prove your case but to support the explanation of the issues that you are presenting to the other side. In considering what to include, see whether the issues appear to be clear to your opponent: parties sometimes surprise you at a very late stage of proceedings by their obvious misunderstanding of your client's position. This is particularly true of the way damages are calculated or argued. Documents that you wish to rely on in supporting your case on quantum should be furnished to the other side well in advance of the mediation hearing. Anything else can be brought with but is unlikely to be needed.

One *caveat* to the minimal documents rule applies, and that is the production and use of expert reports in the mediation. For scientific or technical matters it may be essential for the mediator to develop a working understanding of the problem at hand and the issues dividing the parties, and not possible for him to do so in the absence of such reports. You need to consider whether such reports concern peripheral matters and do not, in fact, go to the core of the dispute between the parties; or whether there are adequate paths to settlement without the mediator or the parties having to consider or resolve the issues for expert evidence which would otherwise have to be proven or disproven at a trial. If it is vital that the mediator deals with the issues being addressed by experts, decide whether a report which may have been prepared for trial is too long or complex, and whether a summary or abstract might suffice. If you adopt this course do not forget that there may be additional documents needed, which are necessary to support the expert opinion upon which you wish to rely.

There will be instances where you have to decide whether the mediator should be asked to read witness statements. You may be better off preparing short summaries of what, it is anticipated, each witness will deal with at the trial. Mediators are unlikely to see the need to read witness statements prepared for trial. However you, as the advocate, must force the issue if you consider it sufficiently important, bearing in mind at all times that you have to prove nothing to the mediator other than that your client is prepared to negotiate a settlement from a position of strength. Ultimately it is for you to decide or agree what the mediator ought to have. He may require very little,

---

[4] If there are a large number of documents consider whether a reading list will assist the mediator.

but you must be confident in asserting what you feel he really needs to see in order to understand the dispute, whether statements of case, core submissions, core documents, an abstract of the witness evidence or full experts' reports.

There may be confidential documents that you wish the mediator to see but not your opponent. These may be sent separately to the mediator prior to the hearing or shown to him in private session.

It is in your client's interest for you to try to agree the minimum documents with your opposing number wherever possible. If you can reach an agreement on the contents of hearing bundles, a timetable, and the format and length of case summaries this should create a momentum and general spirit of agreement in which the participants arrive at the mediation in the right frame of mind.

4.4   The Written Statement of Issues and/or Position Statement for Mediation

Most of the MDCs require the filing of a Statement of Issues which will be used to determine which 'door' is to be used in the court-annexed process. The Statement of Issues will be filed before the ADR Registrar who assigns a Dispute Resolution Officer ('DRO'). This officer will invite the parties to attend a preliminary meeting or screening conference to see whether the dispute is appropriate for disposal by mediation, arbitration, conciliation or early neutral evaluation, and assign the case accordingly. Sometimes this screening process can be done as a paper exercise without the need for parties to attend.

It has generally come to be regarded as an essential feature of pre-mediation preparation that representatives for each party exchange with the others and send to the mediator in good time for the hearing a reasonably concise statement of their client's case and the submissions that they wish to make. The purpose of this document is really threefold: first, to inform the mediator and your opposing party of the live issues in dispute and your client's current position; second, to explain and justify the merits of your client's stance; and third, as a vehicle towards settlement, indicating a willingness to make appropriate concessions and pointing up settlement options.[5]

---

[5] This document should contain as a header or footer: "Without Prejudice - For the Purposes of Mediation Only."

In spite of the need for brevity you will wish to take advantage of the opportunity to make sufficient key points in the written statement of case to persuade the mediator and the other side of the strengths of the case as seen from your own viewpoint. Your opponent will read it and probably his client before the mediation hearing, and, like any piece of effective written advocacy, it should aim to overwhelm the opposing party and deflate his expectation. Therefore you should establish what is the key evidence in support of your client's case, explain why it has force, and why at trial your client is likely to succeed on the merits. You should identify his approach to settlement, rehearse the risks, and can even make an offer or indicate possible concessions.

It is therefore clear that some skill is needed in the preparation of this document. You are not settling a written opening as such, nor is it a pleading or document with a formal structure, but it should contain a number of essential ingredients. Tactically (as we shall see in dealing with the opening statement at the mediation hearing) it is more astute to direct it at the opposing lay party, since it may be the first time this information will have been received without the interference of their lawyers.

I suggest that your Position Statement should contain the following:

1. Identify the Parties *and* the Participants

The mediator does not necessarily know who everyone is, or his or her status. Provide a list of the key personalities he will need to know about and their involvement in the subject matter of the dispute. For ease of reference he may prefer this to be in alphabetical order. This should not be confined to the parties to litigation, or indeed the parties to the dispute. It should extend to anyone having an influence on the outcome, which may include spouses or relatives of individuals, and directors or managers of corporate or institutional parties.

2. The Relevant History

Set out in concise form the relevant history leading up to the dispute. Concise in this instance means what it says – tell the mediator only what he needs to know. This should include any court intervention, finding or relevant part-disposal of any contentious matter.

3. Outline the Dispute

This is a key part of the document. Identify the issues that comprise the whole dispute, or are contextually relevant. Set out those matters that are agreed, not agreed and each party's views.

4. Your Client's Case

Set out your case both as to facts and law, and the nature and extent of the claims as to quantum. (If this is a personal injury claim you should attach an updated schedule of loss.) Identify, as required, those matters of fact and law in dispute between the parties. Where appropriate explain your client's feelings about the conduct of the other side. Show why your client's case on the contested issues is likely to be preferred by a court were the matter to be tried.

5. The Gateway to Settlement

Identify those issues or claims that you believe are capable of being resolved. Explain why your client has agreed to mediation. Deal with any previous settlement history and prior or current offers. Indicate what your client hopes to achieve by the mediation – what are his legal, commercial and personal objectives. Do not close the door to settlement by setting at this stage any limits or pre-conditions. Be constructive and try to dispel any prior aggression between the party's representatives.

6. A Chronology

If the mediator requests one, or if you believe having one may assist the mediator, prepare a chronology. Such a document should be neutral and avoid positional statements, and if possible should be agreed. It should be short and concise providing the key dates and a succinct explanation of major events where necessary. It may help to reduce the number of factual disputes between the parties.

4.5 "Working" with the Mediator in the Pre-Mediation Phase

Advocates should now have enough experience of case management or pre-trial conferences before the judge not to be disconcerted by being telephoned by the mediator in advance of the appointment. What is unusual by comparison with litigation is that a mediator, unlike a judge, can and frequently does contact each side separately beforehand, as he wishes. In training, mediators are encouraged to do so.

The mediation process does not start on the day of the mediation appointment. Most substantial cases will benefit from a preliminary meeting between the mediator and the lawyers involved, or at least an exchange of telephone calls. It is perfectly possible for the mediator to see parties separately in advance should he choose to do so. This is particularly the case where he wants to get an early feel for the players involved, start building a rapport, particularly with the lawyers, or "pick up" on sticky issues or difficult people. Mostly a telephone call will suffice. This is intended as the beginning of a constructive, co-operative process in which the mediator will outline the process and responsibilities of the participants, check the lawyer's mediation experience, confirm who will be in attendance, request such further information as may be necessary, ask how the claim might settle, confirm that settlement authority exists, explore any existing offers, and generate a broader discussion of any likely pitfalls or hindrances to settlement. This information, or the nuances contained in some aspects of it, cannot necessarily be picked up from documents.

The mediator is not restricted to speaking merely to the lawyers involved. He or she may wish to speak directly with those holding authority to settle in order to start an empathic relationship, or to explain the procedure. This illustrates the flexibility of the process in which you are engaged. It also demonstrates that your mindset as a mediation advocate must be different from that of an advocate dealing with a judge in litigation. Any direct approach to your client should also serve at this early stage as a warning about the possibility of your losing control over the client and his case, which is an essential feature of the lawyer/client relationship during litigation, particularly for an advocate.

Making early contact after the mediator is appointed is also your opportunity to demonstrate to him a co-operative attitude. You will need to agree procedural matters with him or her, for example, the timetable for agreeing core documents, a list of issues, and the exchange of case summaries with the other side. Ask him whether you need to send him anything in advance. Make sure he has everything he needs. This begins a process of trust and confidence-building since you will have to trust him to treat all parties equally.

There are a number of common questions that a mediator might ask ahead of the mediation, the answers to which you will be expected to know. For example:

- Why has the dispute not settled so far?

- What concerns do either you or your client have about negotiating with the other side – i.e. why have you chosen to mediate rather than negotiate directly?

- What problems are likely to arise in mediation negotiations?

- What is required of the other side in order to bring about a satisfactory settlement at the mediation?

- What for your client are the consequences of success?

- And what for your client are the consequences of failure?

These are all matters that will assist the mediator to plan ahead, and to an extent force the parties each to reflect on their present position.

The ability to approach the mediator directly is a useful strategic tool. It enables you, on instructions, to provide confidential documents[6] and information to him; to explain issues the way your client sees them; to feed through ideas as to how you think the case might settle; or to indicate the attitude of your lay client or of his insurers. You can also tell the mediator of previous negotiations and offers.

4.6 Decisions as to Strategy

(1) Who Should Attend

At an early stage you will need to consider whether in fact the client needs legal representation at the hearing. There will be few occasions when you conclude that representation is unnecessary but they may occur, for example if your client is an experienced professional or, if a company wishes to use its company secretary or legal or financial director. You may decide that for reasons of strategy and cost a client that you consider strong enough and competent enough to protect his own commercial interests should be permitted to attend himself, having guided him through the procedure, the likely course of the negotiations, and the arguments and methods of persuasion likely to be adopted by the mediator.

If representation is necessary you should decide what the legal team should comprise. A sizeable legal team can undermine the economy of the process, and the opposite party may find it intimidating. The plenary and caucus rooms may suffer undue overcrowding. You may even convey the wrong

---

[6] If you are sending a confidential briefing note to the mediator this should contain a header or footer stating in terms that it is confidential to the mediator only.

message: you may inadvertently overemphasise the importance to your client either of the dispute itself or his need to settle.

Undoubtedly there may be observers and support staff. Pre-eminent law firms are particularly gregarious and never seem to arrive without at least a small army of assistants. While the mediation process is a useful exercise for trainees and pupil barristers to observe, ideally attendance should be kept to a minimum. Always have the courtesy to ask in advance whether trainees or pupils may attend. Their presence may, at the least, have an impact on logistics. Where you are instructed to turn up with a large team you should agree this in advance with the mediator.

Counsel should be employed if he has had extensive contact with the dispute as prior litigation, or if it is likely that he will conduct the trial should the mediation fail: this will enable him to gain knowledge of the nuances of the case he might not grasp from the papers, a feel for potential witnesses, and an insight into the lay client on the other side and his legal team. Counsel should also be engaged if he has particular specialist knowledge of the legal area of the dispute, experience as a mediation advocate or a particular relationship with any client involved (e.g. insurers). The flexibility of the process is such that counsel may be instructed without the attendance of a solicitor. In most smaller cases it will not be cost effective for counsel to attend.

There are rare occasions when the client himself does not have to attend. Such an instance may concern the defendant to a class action in the latter stages of a series of mediations dealing with similar subject matter but different claimants, by which time the defendant's negotiating position and range is already known. Usually, however, the client will attend either as an individual, or as a team that has the relevant knowledge, power to settle, and includes the core personality involved in the dispute, and has directors or officers of equal importance to the other side.

The mediator will require the attendance of all parties necessary to effect a settlement of both the issue at hand and any relevant parallel or wider issues. The advocate must consider with care who needs to attend for his client. Despite your strong advice as to who should be present, not all parties will be able to send a representative with full authority to settle: for example, an innovative solution, which addresses a wider settlement arena than the immediate dispute, may require authority from a director or a board resolution. It may be that a company's finance director is not present and the need for his presence was not envisaged when the mediation commenced. A local authority may need the approval of its finance or treasury committee based on an advice that the settlement is appropriate. A common occurrence is where insurers may be involved and present at the mediation but the insured parties may wish to be discreet about the participation of insurers, or the level of their cover. Often if the proposed settlement is complex it may need to have underlying financial arrangements agreed between banks or guarantors. An advocate needs to be mindful of these possibilities well in advance of the hearing. It will not surprise the experienced mediator to learn at some point during the day that authority to settle is not infinite. However steps must be taken to ensure that authority for any reasonably envisaged settlement is present.

Those individuals who attend the mediation hearing because of their participation in the dispute (rather than its resolution) are not witnesses as such, but tend to be regarded in much the same way. Lawyers still regard mediation as a quasi-trial rather than a managed settlement negotiation, and feel the need to invite the attendance of those who will be witnesses at the trial if the mediation does not succeed. Normally it is not necessary to have those involved with the facts in issue – indeed a resolution can be easier to achieve if they are not involved in mediation – unless they are the principal parties. It is better not to have too many people in attendance. Ideally those attending should be the parties themselves, and, where necessary, a senior representative of a company or entity with authority to settle and/or the insurer. The mediator should be told who will be in attendance and their respective status.

There are other factors to take into account. You must consider with care any personality conflicts of which you are aware. There may be managerial or other same-side conflicts to bear in mind. A common example is the impact on the person who made a contested decision of an analysis of his decision-making. If he is likely to become aggressive or embarrassed if found wrong – will this impact upon the mediation, particularly his desire to settle or have his company settle? The advocate must find the means to remove any potential undercurrent of conflict in the same side before it occurs.

The use of experts at the hearing needs careful thought. There may be fundamental, technical, valuation, tax or accounting issues, the last three being common. Both you and the mediator will want to ensure parity in the use of experts in the sense that neither party should be disadvantaged by imbalance in the use of expert evidence. All expert evidence to be relied upon, even if incomplete or in draft form, should be exchanged before the date of the mediation. Surprises are not conducive to settlement – they will merely cause the other side to walk out. So both sides must know experts are to attend the mediation, their identity and field of expertise, why they are coming and what they will say. Agreement may need to be reached about whether experts or advisers should attend or be on stand by to be called if necessary, or to attend by telephone or videoconference.

(2) Who should be Contactable?

Having a support team at the client's premises or solicitor's offices is very useful. Often during the course of the day, new information or documents can be required which may suddenly become vital during the latter stages of the hearing. These may relate to issues of liability or quantum, or to deal with the workability or impact of creative solutions. It may also be preferable to have interested third parties, for example the insurer, available to provide telephone instructions rather than be present at the mediation. Please remember that mediations may continue long after office hours and if a support team or third party contact is required out of hours arrangements must be made accordingly.

(3) The Role of Attendees

Before attending the mediation lawyers must have a good understanding not only of their own role but that of everyone present, and must ensure their client is equally aware. However strong the client's case appears to be, and however much you wish to protect your client's interests – to the extent of protecting him from what you consider being a bad deal in the context of his legal rights – it is your responsibility to recognise and support the philosophy and objectives of the mediation. Once you are instructed to attend as your client's advocate there is no room for personal cynicism about the process in which you are engaged. Nor will it assist for you to compare the progress of the mediation with that of a trial. If you are unprepared for what is to follow both your and your client's expectations will be seriously challenged, and may be undermined.

As an advocate in mediation you must understand the central participatory role of clients in the process and be ready to:

- Allow the client to speak and to be heard in open and closed sessions. This is central to the dynamic of mediation, even though you may risk losing control of the client, and possibly the situation

- Be a supporter, not just a mouthpiece. There is a considerable amount of hand-holding to be done, particularly where the client's expectation or optimism diminishes

- Focus on interests as opposed to legal rights. Look at the wider picture for settlement options – the legal case should remain just a frame of reference, but settlement need not follow the legal case if the client's true interests are wider or his needs can be met elsewhere

- Manage the client's expectations by acting as 'the agent of reality'[7]

- Act as a constructive negotiator, promoting positive solutions

- Keep open lines of communication in the face of challenging emotions and mistrust, strong feelings, grievances, and issues of credibility

- Take responsibility for the client when his own feelings get the better of him

- Ensure that the momentum is maintained during periods when your side is not in private session with the mediator as he deals with another party.

Your client's role should be equally well defined prior to arriving at the venue. You must work out in advance who is going to do what, and the effect of your client actively participating rather than just sitting and listening throughout the proceedings, as would be the case at a trial. Decide who will make the opening statement and do not assume that automatically it should be you as the advocate. Tactically you can use an emotional client to embarrass the other side or impress on them how sympathetically a judge might react at the trial to receiving this party's evidence. This can be an effective way of showing off a good witness or emphasising favourable facts. A personal injury case may in particular require a demonstration of the nature of the disability, and this can be of considerable impact if shown by someone who will clearly be a good witness.

In any event your client's active participation will bring home to him or her that this is the day in court, and this is the opportunity to give vent to his feelings about the matter in a controlled but otherwise unrestricted way.

---

[7] Nesic, Miryana *Mediation advocacy: how to keep it on track for results* Paper delivered at CEDR First Mediators' Congress 20 November 2003.

The opening remarks can be split between advocate and client, or even advocate, client and expert. Whatever the decision, the division of active roles should be planned well in advance and the contents well prepared.

As to the role of experts who are asked to be present it is quite likely the mediator will have in mind how they should be used. He will probably ask experts to meet privately and separately, after any contribution they may have made in open session, and produce some jointly agreed parameters which can be used on a without prejudice basis to assist settlement strategies.

Do not forget that some clients may wish just to sit and listen, and take no active role until actively encouraged to do so by the mediator. Even then they may assume that representing their case is what you are being paid for. An experienced mediator will know how to draw the parties into active participation, and sometimes on a level that may make you feel superfluous, although you must do your best to stifle that feeling if progress is obviously being made towards a resolution of the dispute.

(4) Preparing the Attendees

It follows from the foregoing suggestions that it is advisable that you arrange a pre-mediation conference with the lay client for him to understand precisely what mediation involves. The client should assemble all of the information necessary for his representatives to understand not only the dispute but also any commercial or wider interests that require protection or advancement. At the conference the client and his legal team can then begin to consider what he is trying to achieve and how he wishes to negotiate. To that end at least one decision maker must be involved at the earliest stages of preparation. It is important to establish the difference between 'needs' and 'wants.' The opportunity should also be taken to determine the difference between the client's best alternative to a negotiated agreement ('BATNA') and his worst alternative to a negotiated agreement ('WATNA'). A detailed risk analysis is a good way to prepare for both negotiations and to reduce expectations, particularly those held by persons in a higher managerial, corporate or institutional tier than those personally involved with the facts in dispute, and to diffuse any previously held aggressive or other strong emotions. You as the lawyer should apply rigorous logic when comparing the litigation risk with any proposed commercial solution.

The advocate should also take the time to explain the tactics that a mediator might employ in relation to the parties, their lawyers and their experts. He must ascertain exactly what technical or legal assistance will be required.

Make aware to all who are to attend that normally a mediation appointment can be a very long day. Any movement towards settlement is initially very slow, and it may take a long time to start. The momentum tends to pick up as the day ends but there can be large obstructions over small issues near the end of a concluded settlement, and these may run well into the evening. In addition any agreement reached must be reduced to writing and signed by the parties before they leave. Everyone should know that it is quite common for this stage to be long after nightfall, including well after the last train or normal bus home.

To that end legal representatives should not undermine the process by announcing that they have tickets for a football match and will be leaving at 5.00 pm. It is unprofessional, and potentially an act bringing their profession into disrepute. Experienced advocates should be aware that mediation appointments are usually not time limited and should certainly make no other professional or social arrangements following a mediation. If that is the client's choice, so be it, but it should not be yours.

Unlike litigation there are no strictures on formal rehearsal or the training of parties for what is in store. A useful exercise to conduct for your client is to bring together everyone involved in the dispute and divide them into two teams to rehearse the entire negotiation strategy, with one team arguing for your client and the other against. Be curious about the other side's bargaining position. Do not assume you know their view of the strengths and weaknesses of their case, or their underlying interests. You are unlikely to know anything of their personalities. But you can try and put yourself in their position to ascertain their client's needs and interests

The client must be encouraged to keep an open mind about the process and its likely outcome, and therefore to be flexible about his expectations. These should not be absolute; he should have a negotiating range not a fixed position. The same can be said for each of the participants on your side, particularly insurers. Getting the participants into the right frame of mind is part of the mediation advocate's task. If there is travel involved in getting to the venue, suggest a relaxed dinner in the hotel the night before.

(5) Ethics and Other Matters

There are a number of other matters you should consider either yourself or together with your client in a pre-mediation conference, apart from dispute-specific items. These concern aspects of your professional relationship with your opponent, or the opposing party if he is unrepresented, and the mediator, namely how you intend to discharge your role during the mediation. At a trial an advocate's approach and conduct is governed by the substantive procedural rules of the relevant jurisdiction, specific case management directions, the law of evidence and his obligations to the Court[8] and to the governing or regulatory bodies of his profession. Subject to the disciplinary sanctions for conduct unbecoming a solicitor or barrister, the only rules governing an advocate's conduct at a mediation are those contained in the relevant MDC Practice Directions[9], or, in the private sector, the mediation agreement as terms and conditions of that contract, or otherwise agreed between the parties and the mediator as a matter of procedure.

There are no rules of evidence. The advocate is engaged to protect or enhance the client's interests in settling the dispute by whatever means he may consider expedient, professional and proper. This freedom may conflict with the extent to which either he, on instructions, or his client is completely candid with the mediator or with the other side in presenting his client's case or negotiating stance. The ethical dilemma for lawyers is still something of a grey area and the subject of some ongoing debate, however the bottom line is that conduct during a mediation, which brings the reputation of a profession into disrepute, is likely to attract a disciplinary sanction. For the Bar, a barrister instructed in a mediation must not knowingly or recklessly mislead the mediator or any party or their representative.

There is also a financial incentive for the lawyer. For example, Order 4 r.17 of the FCT Rules states that

> a certificate of pre-action counselling signed by counsel and the litigant shall be filed along with the writ where proceedings are initiated by counsel, showing that the parties have been appropriately advised as to the relative strength or weakness of their respective cases, and the counsel shall be personally liable to pay the cost of the proceeding where it turns out to be frivolous.

The import of this rule is to place a responsibility on counsel to advise the client on the proper mechanism to use when instructed. Rather than litigate, counsel is expected to advise his client appropriately that the matter warrants

---

[8] *Vernon v Bosely (No 2)* [1999] QB 18 CA.
[9] These envisage that counsel will give regard to and ensure that clients accord respect to notices, invitations and directives from the MDC; to ensure the attendance of his client at every mediation session; to explore with the client options for the speedy conclusion of the mediation; to respect confidentiality; to embrace a cultural change and accept an advisory role while the parties take the lead role in mediation sessions; and be co-operative and encourage his client to be co-operative during the mediation sessions.

consideration of the use of ADR/mediation. Where the issues at stake lean towards a reconciliation of the interest of parties then litigating will serve no purpose, and it may be that full mediation may also be unnecessary.

For practical purposes, when discussing in conference the tactical approach to adopt in the forthcoming negotiation, either with the opposite party or the mediator, it is as well to keep in mind the following:

(i)   The mediator succeeds because he operates on the basis of a relationship of trust. Each party reposes their trust in him, and for his part he must assume that what he is told, particularly what he is told in confidence, or is told to advance to the other side, is truthful. A breakdown of trust in the mediator is likely to cause the mediation to fail. Should you break faith with him he will find it difficult to continue to represent your position to the other parties.

(ii)   If the opposing party is unhappy or uncomfortable or aggrieved at your negotiating style or position, he may simply walk away at any time. This is very likely if your opponent believes you to be disingenuous.

(iii)   Mediated agreements may be set aside by the courts for being induced by misrepresentation[10] in the same way as any other contract,[11] and with all the consequences that will necessarily flow from such an eventuality.

4.7 What Does The Client Want To Achieve?

The pre-mediation conference with a lay client should establish precisely what outcome is needed, not just in relation to the legal cause of action or defence, but taking into account the full range of wider commercial, relationship, personal and emotional interests where present. One effective way of doing this is to list out everything the client is interested in achieving and then prioritising these by dividing them into categories. I suggest that the categories be ranked 'needs' 'would like' 'nice to have' and the items within each category ranked with a value: see Figure 3 overleaf. Once the list has

---

[10] *Vedatech Corpn v Crystal Decision UK Ltd and Crystal Decision (Japan) KK* [2003] EWCA Civ 1066.

[11] Foskett QC, David *The Law and Practice of Compromise* Thomson Sweet & Maxwell 6th edn 2005 4-37/4-50.

been compiled with values attached, it is useful exercises to anticipate the other side's list, attributing such values as you believe are appropriate. The differences in value will give rise to bargaining, with hopefully, each side having matters to which they attribute less value being available to trade, with the recipient attributing greater value in their hands.

This notion of looking for 'differences' which may be traded is a common strategy of the mediator, and a task for the advocate is to try and use the mediator to ascertain the true values within the other side's list. An experienced mediator will use this process, but not reveal such information.

A similar approach may be to compile in advance matters/items/issues that might be given away (see Figure 4).

Apparent single issue cases should be broken down into smaller items: a payment of money as the issue can be divided into several issues by the application of time, so that it includes having to consider and agree the amount, the nature of the payment i.e. a single transfer or tranches; if the latter, how many and over what period; any discounting; any interest; any provision for default; provision for costs; any confidentiality attaching to the settlement. Thus what appears to be a sole issue can be converted in to eight for the purpose of bargaining.

Fig 3. Preparation of a prioritised List of Needs and Interests

Own Client	Client's Perception of Other Side's view of Us	Client's perception of Other Side	Other Side Actual (Discover at Mediation)
We need	They think we need	We think they need	They need
1.	1.	1.	1.
2.	2.	2.	2.
3.	3.	3.	3.
4.	4.	4.	4.
We Would Like	They think we would like	We think they would like	They Would Like
5.	5.	5.	5.
6.	6.	6.	6.
7.	7.	7.	7.
8.	8.	8.	8.
Happy to have	They think we might want	We think they might want	They're happy to have
9.	9.	9.	9.
10.	10.	10.	10.
11.	11.	11.	11.
12.	12.	12.	12.

Fig 4. Preparation of a prioritised Bargaining List for Negotiation

Own Client	Client's Perception of Other Side's view of Us
We will give	They think we will give
1.	1.
2.	2.
3.	3.
4.	4.
We might give	They think we might give
5.	5.
6.	6.
7.	7.
8.	8.
We will not give	They think we will not give
9.	9.
10.	10.
11.	11.
12.	12.

4.8 Obtaining Authority to Settle

It is an essential requirement of the process that all sides come to the mediation with authority to settle, and the mediation agreement will usually specify that this is so. *All persons who have to approve the settlement* should ordinarily be present at the mediation session, and where the settlement is subject to approval by a higher authority, that higher authority must attend and see the process, otherwise he will not be affected by the dynamic which propels the parties towards the agreement: any party external to the mediation may need to be persuaded that the settlement figure is justified. Moreover this means the parties themselves have authority, and not just their legal advisers, unless the latter are fully authorised to settle.

The lawyer should be prepared for probing in advance about any limit of his or his client's authority to settle. The mediator may well wish to receive a formal acknowledgement from the lawyer that his authority extends to the full amount of the Claim. If in fact the settlement authority is limited, you should ensure that the limit extends at least beyond offers previously made and rejected. The mediator may also require specific information about settlement authority to be given from third parties, an obvious example being an insurer's reserve.

An advocate does not discharge his duty, will certainly ensure the mediation shall fail, and may well be guilty of professional misconduct, if:

(1)   he fails to come to mediation with appropriate authority e.g. the decision-maker does not attend, or his authority is wholly inadequate and he fails to advise the mediator about authority problems;

(2)   he misrepresents to the mediator the level of his authority; or

(3)   he represents at the mediation he has no authority as a tactic to buy time or to impose negotiation pressure on the other side.

A mediation advocate must never overlook authority issues. Even if he is confident about his client's authority to settle, towards the end of the mediation the considerable and perhaps unexpected movement that often takes place can be derailed by one side lacking necessary authority. The settlement itself may easily be jeopardised. Therefore if you cannot make sure that the client has the means to meet a settlement because the momentum of the process is running away and there may be some circumstance where it is not possible to obtain authority e.g. a board approval is required, at least indicate in good faith when the authority will be made available, come clean about the problem as early as possible, and have the courage to suspend the proceedings if you judge it necessary to do so.

4.9 Working up The Mediation 'Brief'

Preparing for the mediation appointment itself is no less onerous a task for the advocate than getting up a brief for trial, although it will be different since the emphasis will be on establishing the client's wider needs and interests and investing time in creating a negotiating strategy. He or she must know the legal case, including all the pertinent facts and witnesses involved or likely to be so; be fully conversant with all of the important and contested legal and factual issues, having identified and analysed them; and be able to list the strengths and weaknesses of both sides. This requirement is almost a constant since one of the principal roles of the mediation advocate is to be able to make comparison with the legal frame of reference ("The Box" in Figure 1[12]) and so keep a close eye on the offer on the table, and the client's best alternative to a negotiated agreement (BATNA).[13]

He or she will usually be asked to prepare and deliver a brief opening statement. This is not a repetition of the written position statement and the advocate should try to find something new to say.

Although the mediation advocate does not have to plan the examination and cross-examination of witnesses, he should formulate tough questions for the mediator to take to the other side in the caucus sessions to reality test during the exploration phase of the mediation, and to reduce the expectation of the party opposite. I shall say more about adversarial and collaborative strategies later.[14]

Unlike a trial brief the mediation advocate has to work out in some detail his settlement or negotiation strategy. He must have opening settlement positions on both liability and quantum. He should have identified those imponderable factors that might cause his starting point to come under

---

[12] See p.16.
[13] See pp.107.
[14] See pp.109-120.

pressure, for example new or clarified information, or the impact of the other side appearing more cogent or compelling than anticipated.

The mediation advocate should be aware of what his client will eventually be prepared to settle for. He must be primed with a negotiating strategy enabling him to know how to get to where he wants. In order to do this he will have considered where negotiations stand now, and have taken instructions or given advice on a realistic settlement range.

As a consequence he should keep away from founding an offer or making a demand based on the age of the case or its current progress in litigation. If he can identify the best likely outcome for his client, the advocate should try to ascertain what offers or demands will get his client within range of that outcome, and then move in that direction.

At all times during his final preparation the advocate should know:

- What are the real prospects of success at trial;
- What is the real value of claim;
- What are the particular needs, if any, of the client;
- What result would be in his best interest.

Other commentators[15] have suggested there is a benefit to be obtained from having a checklist for final preparation.

Any checklist should include the following steps:

(1) Review all the files and know what evidence supports the case: what are the witnesses, core documents, expert reports and real evidence? Ensure you have all the information necessary for a final evaluation of the case.

(2) Know what heads of damage are claimed: is quantum justified or supported for each?

(3) Prepare calculations of interest down to the mediation, and then to an expected trial date.

---

[15] See in particular Nesic, Miryana *Mediation* Tottel 2001; Dodson, Charles *Preparing for Mediation* CEDR Resolutions issue 17 Summer 1997.

(4) Know what assertions of law are to be advanced on (i) liability and (ii) damages, with supporting relevant, recent authority. In evaluating the legal case the mediator may put the two lawyers together to thrash out the legal position, or may wish to challenge your own view of the law.

(5) List out the particular strengths and weaknesses in your case.

(6) List the particular strengths and weaknesses in your opponent's case.

(7) Set out the costs to date of your own side, the expected costs of the other side, and the anticipated costs of both parties from here to the end of the trial. Make sure you go into the mediation appointment knowing your client's breakdown of costs to date and any revisions to costs estimates, and calculate the likely irrecoverable element. Get the other side to produce theirs, either by a direct request or through the mediator. It is vital he knows what they are.

(8) Review the mediation procedure - know what to expect.

(9) Confirm the attendance of all necessary participants involved in the mediation, and that the necessary authority to settle is available – the dispute cannot settle otherwise

(10) Mull over your negotiation strategy and refine it: know what compensation or restitution is possible; what plans for future action are practicable; how emotional or psychological issues can be dealt with; and how to 'expand the pie' by identifying opportunities that will be of benefit to both sides, e.g. costs savings, tax savings, time and opportunity cost savings, restoration or preservation of commercial, social or family relationships.

(11) Consider whether the settlement aimed for has any necessary financial, tax or technical implications that might give rise either to authority problems or potentially cause a settlement agreement to be delayed.

(12) Settle the formal parts of a stay Order if the matter is in litigation or settlement agreement i.e. parties, recitals, anticipated settlement clauses.

(13)   Ensure that you have available everything that you will need on the day of the mediation appointment:

(a) calculator

(b) lap-top computer

(c) mobile phone

(d) important contact numbers

(e) case summaries/position statements

(f) agreed documents bundle

(g) other documents to be made available if referred to

(h) schedule of damages

(i) interest calculation

(j) costs breakdown

(k) note of opening

(l) counsel's opinions

(m) draft stay Order including, where appropriate, draft confidentiality clause.

4.10 Pre-Appointment Preparation

It will be plain by now from the tenor of this book that mediation is not merely a negotiating process that requires little or no preparation. Do not let a lawyer's natural cynicism assume that the mediation appointment will merely be a horse-trading session. It follows from the preceding section that your client's case must be mastered and prepared in the ordinary way: it may not be presented or run in a trial format in the sense that you are trying to prove your case before an impartial but decision-making tribunal, but the intellectual considerations are just the same. Both lay and professional clients will not appreciate it if you are seen to have been casual in your preparation.

In proffering advice on the tactics and procedure you wish your client to use in the mediation you must be in a position to explain the process and the roles of each of the participants (Note – the 'participants', not merely the 'parties'). You must be able to advise your client where it is the case:

- Not to have absolute expectations – his case will be the subject of reality testing both by the mediator in private meetings, or caucuses, and by the other side in open or plenary sessions.

- To know what he wants to achieve in terms of priorities: he must be comfortable with what is essential and what is an ideal, whether a monetary settlement or otherwise (see Fig.3 at page 75 above).

- To deal with the realities of the situation as it may change during the mediation, otherwise he may face winning a Pyrrhic victory.

And you should make it clear that:

- He is able to treat the mediation as his 'day in court', participating actively to make all the points about which he is concerned.

- The ambit of settlement options is not constrained by either strict legal merits or litigation procedure, and he can look elsewhere for goals he wants to achieve, including non-monetary goals, and matters outside the present dispute.

- Procedurally, there is a possibility that separate meetings may occur within the mediation, e.g. between the two lawyers only, or the experts, lay clients', accountants, or directors as the mediator considers appropriate and the parties agree.

4.11 The Advice on Mediation for the Client

If called upon to prepare written advice for your client dealing with the mediation, whether formal or informal, the contents will necessarily be different from an opinion on the legal or evidential merits of a case in litigation, or its potential outcome in terms of quantum.

At the legal level of the dispute, you will of course want to assess the cause of action or defence in terms of its merits and quantum. To that end you will summarise the facts of the case, the legal issues, and the evidence available; you will consider your client's prospects in terms of the quantum of damage likely to be recovered, and discuss any other relief required, including its enforceability, perhaps evaluating the best and worst case outcomes and what percentage chance of each is probable. You may wish to factor in any available choice of process or particular timescale. Certainly costs liability will be an important consideration in view of the exercise of the court's discretion.

However, unlike an advice in litigation, your analysis of the client's position does not stop there. There are two further levels[16] of the dispute that need to be taken into account in providing an advice on mediation. Beyond the strictly legal analysis there is a commercial level to the dispute. You have to understand what commercial arrangement reflects the client's needs and interests, and see what, if any, commercial solutions are available and suitable that might take into account past and future business opportunities involving the parties.

There is also a personal level to the dispute that may be of great importance to your client. You need to contemplate and advise how the client can obtain personal closure and move on with his life. He is not able to secure one of the benefits of a litigated outcome – in court he may have the satisfaction of a judge telling him he was right, although conversely he risks the court's disapproval of his actions, or he may win or lose only on a legal technicality. To resolve any personal issues the client needs a process of catharsis, and experienced mediators will be alive to this and use it as a path to settlement.

To advise properly upon the conduct and potential outcome of the litigation you must have a clear view of what you want to achieve. Is a monetary settlement all your client wants? What are his priorities? What objectives are essential and what are an ideal? Your client will have to deal with the realities of the situation so you must know what these are, and in doing so you will come to see what range of proposals you can make.

4.12 Fixing the Mediation Appointment

Once the decision to mediate has been taken and a mediator has been appointed the appointment should be fixed as soon as reasonably possible. The mediator will generally be chosen according to his or her diary commitments with a view to mediating within a relatively short time period, and that is presumably the basis upon which practitioners will be appointed to the designated panels of neutrals. Since key benefits to the client are the intended savings in costs and time when compared to running the dispute in litigation, you need to take advantage of the momentum of the parties having agreed to mediate and having agreed the particular mediator's appointment.

---

[16] See: *Mediation Advocacy – How to keep it on track for results* Miryana Nesic, Hammonds, seminar at the First CEDR Mediator's Congress, London, November 2003.

If litigation is running it is important to suspend the running of time in the action and to stop the costs clock by halting any wider investigatory, disclosure or other procedural work. In the meantime you can run the mediation as a limited, self-contained entity for the purpose of costs.

While there is certainly a strong element of pre-appointment preparation to be dealt with, and occasionally pre-appointment meetings or dealings with the mediator, generally you should aim at a delay of no longer than three to four weeks between the appointment of the mediator and the mediation itself. Often a factor in agreeing the mediator, or his services being procured by a mediation services provider, is his availability. Arguably getting an early date for the mediation is more important than worrying about preparation time. If you are aware that extensive preparation will be required, or the attendance of key personnel or experts that is a different matter and the appointment will have to be delayed. But once the decision to mediate has been made, the process should be driven forward and not allowed to lapse by inactivity.

4.13 Getting it Wrong

There are undoubtedly lawyers who find themselves having to represent clients at mediations and who, while not openly hostile to the concept, are antipathetic and disapproving. They are either reluctant, or too lazy or ignorant about mediation procedures to commit to what is required of them. This ambivalence towards a process which most agree should succeed more often than fail, leads to bad personal lawyering habits which undermine the dynamic and will put the client at a real disadvantage. Either the mediation will fail when it may well have led to settlement, or the client will actually walk away with a smaller settlement or a greater feeling of dissatisfaction than should have been the case

The most significant of these bad habits is poor preparation – not having on the day an adequate grasp of the facts, evidence, law, the party's true interests, the settlement options available, and sufficient knowledge of the costs. This undermines the possibility of making the client aware of his best and worst alternatives to a negotiated agreement.

By way of contrast, some advocates adopt entirely the wrong approach with their preparation by getting up the case as if it were for a trial, that is, by assuming they have to 'prove' to the mediator or persuade him their client's case is better than that of the other side. This leads to the inclusion of too much material, and either using documents for their probative value rather than as a vehicle for settlement, or being wary about which documents to disclose to the mediator for fear of waiver of privilege or their misuse.

Some advocates dismiss mediation as a simple 'horse trading' exercise, when in reality the process is much more sophisticated than they can see, and in this respect they fail to take advantage of what is now a highly developed and skilled exercise in meeting their client's true needs, or if particularly fortunate, gaining their client's desires.

Other practical problems created by inexperienced or ambivalent representation include:

(i)   Failing to involve all of the relevant parties in the mediation, or all of the parties outside the litigation; had all relevant parties been involved this might have unlocked the settlement by assisting with the wider interests of the parties

(ii)   Failing to identify who should be present at the mediation itself, e.g. the insurer who will fund or the technician who might be needed to implement the solution – a person with relevant financial (e.g. tax) or technical (e.g. conveyancing) knowledge, peripheral to the main argument but important to any practical solution.

(iii)   Bringing in inappropriate or difficult persons – persons close to the dispute who have too much self-interest to protect, either within hierarchical establishments or other employment contexts, to be useful.

(iv)   Bringing in the wrong person – for example, a manager without sufficient knowledge of the dispute, who can make no positive contribution to the proceedings.

A lawyer or other mediation representative who has a negative attitude about the process or about being there, will not be difficult to spot. He is likely to display unfamiliarity with the procedure and uncertainty over the lawyer's role or the behaviour of the mediator. He will monopolise the private sessions giving his client no chance to air private thoughts or grievances. He may well adopt the stance (or reveal his belief and advise) that to apologise or express regret is an admission of liability, express concern about having to compromise on a matter of principle, exaggerate the need to preserve face or avoid loss of face (including his own rather that that of his client), give wildly optimistic advice to his client and over rely on his initial advice.

Such a representative is a liability: he sees only what he wants to see; he finds it difficult to acknowledge or understand his client's loss, anger or frustration; he does not consider it his role to deal with the client's goals or non-legal risks, e.g. the impact of litigation bringing adverse publicity, irretrievable lost management time, and other hidden costs. Such a lawyer concentrates on legal questions and may miss entirely the important commercial interests, not only of his client, but those of the other side that might prompt an advantageous settlement. He is the sort of advocate who will use vague language and clichéd expressions in the mediation, such as, 'there are no guarantees,' or 'who knows what the judge will do'- when he should be specific and advise his client about the risks involved in litigation.

Equally dangerous is the lawyer who is too sure of himself. He neglects relevant information. He ridicules good suggestions because they have been made by the other side or by the mediator. He may consider that his client has already invested too much time and money in the conflict to settle in mediation; or he may have given bullish advice before and be fearful of challenging his own client in a private session to re-adjust the unrealistic expectations held by the client which are likely to be exposed by the process as it continues.

A lawyer may properly be fearful of giving advice because it is too early and he needs more facts and evidence before he can make an appropriate assessment. If so he should ensure that mediation only occurs when the time is right.

The ambivalent, uncertain or unprepared mediation advocate may become antagonistic or emotionally involved in the dispute. Or he may consider that settlement in mediation is a purely commercial matter for the client in which he does not need to participate as a lawyer. This is true of that breed of litigator who sees himself as a hired gun and finds it difficult to assume a conciliatory role even as a negotiator.

The answer seems to be whatever your personal thoughts about mediation, put the client's interests first. You can only do this by:

- Keeping an open mind;

- Forming an understanding of the process;

- Learning about the procedure;

- Being prepared in all aspects of your case;

- Understanding that the legal framework of the dispute may be only one aspect of the parties' interests;

- Being receptive to solutions which are outside the legal framework of the dispute;

- Using the mediator as a tool with which to obtain a benefit for your client, rather than seeing him as an obstacle.

If you adopt this approach you will not only engage properly with the process, your client will benefit from the holistic, healing approach with which mediation is concerned:- to give your client control of his problem, help him find a desirable solution to it, and enable him to draw a line and move on with his life.

PART 5

The Mediation Appointment

Chapter 5

THE MEDIATION APPOINTMENT

5.1 Timetabling

In the UK civil/commercial mediation model most mediation appointments last a day. Complex or multi-party cases may last two or three days, but even in very high value claims it would be unusual for a mediation to last for much longer. This contrasts with the 'Harvard' model used by the ICC and others, and by Family Mediators in this jurisdiction, which are based on a series of fixed appointments which may last a period of weeks, and in which there is very little private caucusing. This model seems to have been adopted in Kaduna.

Commercial time limited mediation schemes can last for four or five hours and be fixed by agreement. In such cases the time is usually only fixed in relation to the mediator's or mediation service provider's fee, which may be topped up at an hourly rate thereafter.

Do not expect the mediation will finish within the set time frame: it is notoriously difficult to concertina the time required for the process to succeed to the satisfaction of the parties into a mere three hours.

Mediations commonly run well into the night, and certainly after close of normal business hours. Mediators will generally take advantage of the 'locked-room syndrome' or the fear of missing last transport links to focus the parties' minds on settlement, or at least overcome the last hurdles. Being under pressure of time impacts on the settlement dynamics – either the client or his lawyer feels he must go or the pressure of time makes the settlement ultimately unsatisfactory when considered with hindsight. Therefore make sure you leave enough time in your schedule: do not fix afternoon meetings or conferences; do not expect to get away for social activities in the early evening. There is little more unprofessional than a representative sabotaging mediation by needing to leave. Mediators may well invite the lay party to continue in his or her absence. Warn your client of the possible length of the appointment and to come prepared for a very long day.

Even when agreement has been reached it may still take some time for a document incorporating the heads of agreement to be prepared. The mediator will not allow the lawyers to depart without having done so, since he will not risk the settlement becoming unravelled if the parties have second thoughts on the way home.

Allow for substantial periods of inactivity during the day when the mediator may be elsewhere and you have completed any tasks set for you and your client in his absence. You should constantly finesse your negotiating position, adapting to any additional information or change affecting your client. The client should be advised to bring something else to do, or to read. You should not, unless your client is absent.

5.2 Practical Considerations

Make sure of the due appointment, familiarise yourself with the location of the mediation, and ensure that you arrive on time. If you are visiting an unfamiliar venue allow time to park, and to unload and carry any necessary files and materials to the venue. Being late sends a wrong message. If possible arrive about 30 minutes early to meet the mediator and client and establish a base in the room in which your client's private sessions will be conducted.

Although you will have burdened the mediator beforehand with as little as possible, take with you to the mediation all files, copies of any documents intended for the other side, writing materials, a laptop, mobile telephone, and portable printer if you have one. Consider the use of visual aids pertinent to the issues, which may make it easier to carry your points to the mediator and the opposite party. If you are going to produce documents to the other side that they have not yet seen, hand them out after any explanation you need to give, not beforehand.

5.3 Procedure

Although a key feature of mediation is its flexibility, where the parties are free to choose their own procedure with the guidance of the mediator, a standard procedure has evolved.

Irrespective of the venue, the mediator is, in effect, the host. He or she will meet and greet the parties, explain the facilities and give guidance on the day's proceedings. This introductory meeting is important as it will usually be the first opportunity most of the participants have to meet the mediator. Some mediators take their time over these preliminary meetings, seeking information or clarification, engaging with the parties to start to build a relationship of confidence and trust, exploring the format of the opening joint session, and where necessary, encouraging or even cajoling reluctant parties to join and participate in that meeting.

The parties and their representatives will first be asked to read through and sign the mediation agreement, either in the privacy of their own rooms or at the commencement of the opening session. The mediator will then sign that document himself. This feature of private dispute processing is of itself unusual, since the mediator is likely to have been acting de facto under the terms of the mediation agreement for days, if not a few weeks, prior to its execution by all parties since he will have a copy signed by the parties individually. Under most MDC procedure the mediation agreement will have been signed and returned to the ADR Registrar or DRO.

The Joint Session or 'Plenary'

At the beginning of the opening joint session, after everyone in the room has introduced themselves, the mediator will give a short introduction to the procedure and the approximate timetable in which he will explain his function. Most mediators will take this opportunity to explain a little of their own background and experience and make certain key points:

- That the process is voluntary and the parties are free to leave if they choose;

- That the entire process is confidential and without prejudice to the extent the law permits,[1] and will remain so unless or until a settlement agreement is reached;

- That within the confidentiality of the whole process the contents of the private sessions are separately confidential and will not be disclosed to the other side unless the mediator is expressly permitted to do so;

- That the parties are expected to have settlement authority.

The mediator will also encourage the parties by acknowledging the progress they have made in merely attending the hearing; he will probably caution them not to read anything into his choice of the order in which he sees the parties privately or the relative length of any private sessions.

---

[1] See Part 6.

Essentially the open meeting is client-centred. The seating should be the mediator, then a lay client either side of him, and then the lawyers and outside of them any experts, supporting 'witnesses' and observers, including third party decision makers. This is intended to contrast with litigation where in all hearings the lawyer is placed between the judge and the opposing parties.

The mediator will invite an opening statement of about 5 - 10 minutes from the legal representatives of each party directed at the other party, not the mediator, followed by a short statement from each lay client. He will stress that these statements must be uninterrupted, and should be listened to carefully. The statements may result in a discussion. The mediator will generally summarise the parties' respective positions.

After the opening session the parties retire to separate rooms. The mediator will then move from room to room, speaking with the parties, until there is either resolution or deadlock. He explores with each party the strengths and weaknesses of its or their case and the quantum, risks, and costs implications. He will want to know each party's wider aspirations for a successful outcome, and try to assess what each regards as most important. Even if he is not evaluative the mediator is hardly passive. He will probe your contentions and expectations. At the end of each private session or caucus he will review what he has been told and clarify what he may reveal to the other side, including any offers. He will want to know about any previous settlement proposals and on what basis they were calculated and rejected.

The mediator may at some stage invite the parties to return to a joint open session, so that a direct explanation or presentation of a particular point can be made, and if there is a particular difficulty. He may fragment the parties' teams by having the experts, the lawyers, or the decision-makers meet entirely separately, either simultaneously or consecutively. On the other hand the mediator may decide for good reason to have no further joint meeting after the opening session.

The mediation hearing will be concluded in one of three ways: there will be a concluded agreement; there will be an insuperable difficulty causing one or both sides to withdraw; or the time available may expire with the parties adjourning the mediation to be continued on another occasion.

Where there is a settlement the lawyers will settle the necessary agreement in as much detail as possible and those present with the requisite authority will sign it before leaving. If one or both of the parties withdraw the mediator may have to make a report to that effect to the mediation service provider or, where it is a court-annexed mediation, to the court. The mediator will only report the fact of failure and is not entitled to apportion blame or the court to investigate it.[2]

If the time available for the appointment expires the parties may wish to assess whether there is sufficient momentum in the negotiations to continue without a mediator. It may take a little time for the client and his lawyers to assess the position. If the mediator is still required a further session should be arranged as soon as reasonably practicable after the first. In the family and Harvard mediation models a series of appointments are booked, rather than trying to conclude a settlement within a day.

5.4 The Opening Statement

Presenting the opening statement in mediation is unlike making opening submissions to a judge at trial. However strange it feels, the advocate should address the opposite party directly and not the mediator. At this early stage his aim is to provide information about his client's concerns, not to negotiate or altercate or to propose or accept solutions.

Unlike a trial there is no formal structure. The mediator decides who goes first. Invariably it will be the claimant, but not always. Most importantly you should be aware that there is usually no right of reply, although unlike a court hearing the mediator will now customarily invite the parties to speak personally after or in addition to the lawyers.

Do not waste the opportunity presented by the invitation to give an opening statement: the mediator will ask the other side to listen to you without interruption, and focus on what you are saying.[3] There are few opportunities in contentious work to be able to address directly a decision maker on the other side without interruption. Make full use of it.

Prepare and, if you can, practice the opening statement before the session. This will aid conciseness and accuracy. Brevity is important. Be concise and business like. If you haven't before, introduce your team. Then provide an uncluttered, unemotional focus on the core issues, not minutiae, dealing with your client's current needs – not past obsessions or grievances. Do not

---

[2] See *Venture Investment Placement Ltd v Hall* [2005] EWHC 1227 (Ch). In subsequent costs proceedings the court may not investigate or make a finding why the mediation did not succeed.
[3] Anecdotal evidence suggests that imaginative openings that grab the party's attention are often very effective.

include much history unless it is directly relevant to the present settlement process. Do not refer to documents unless you consider it absolutely vital to do so. On the other hand, a visual aid, such as a chart or diagram, might hold the attention of the opposing side and make it easier to explain either a complicated or a technical position. At the commencement or conclusion you should assert your client's desire to work towards a settlement or some such positive statement. You will already have decided in advance who will be present at the first and any subsequent joint session. If it is tactically advantageous divide the presentation between those who should deal with the law, the facts, and emotive or technical issues. You may wish to encourage your client to deal with his commercial imperatives or emotional concerns, and can expect the mediator to encourage personal exchanges. Letting the client give vent to his feelings is what the mediator wishes to happen. You, as the advocate, need to decide on their likely impact and potential importance. It may be the only time that your client can says precisely what he wants in the way he wants to say it. Of course it may not be, but your client should still be given the opportunity to express his version and understanding of events, unless you consider it would be disastrous to permit him to do so.

In preparing the contents of your opening statement consider each of the following items:

(i)   How briefly to deal with the history of the matter: cut out all unnecessary detail; where possible focus on the present situation and the future rather than the past.

(ii)   How to summarise the main points of the dispute between the parties as you see them, using broad themes: go over the facts of the case, indicating areas of agreement and disagreement and the available evidence. Explain your analysis of liability and damages based on the facts of the case; if you are responding, say why you disagree with your opponent's statement of case. Analyse any different levels at which the conflict operates, including substantive law and the risk to the respective parties in either commercial or personal terms against their desire to end the litigation.

(iii)   How best to outline what you want to achieve in the mediation: avoid specific settlement figures at the outset and speak in general terms. Avoid emotive language but explain the impact of the dispute on your client. Suggest what decisions need to be made at the mediation.

You will need to be realistic. While emphasising your strengths and presenting your case in the most favourable way, do not ignore its weaknesses. Tell the other side if you have already factored weaknesses into a previous offer, or at least that you are conscious of the weaker points of your case for the purpose of negotiation.

Select language and a style of presentation that will engage the opposing party in what you are saying - tell them that which will keep their attention – and do not cause them to switch off by telling them what they do not want to hear. Be positive – explain that you wish to have a settlement that will satisfy both sides.

After you have concluded your own presentation listen carefully and without interruption to what the other side are saying in their opening. Do not be dismissive. Get the client to listen carefully – he may well be hearing something for the first time or something he has not appreciated or realised before. It is such revelations that break the logjam of previously held entrenched positions. If he is cynical try to ensure that he does not express his cynicism with facial or other gestures that are likely to alienate or antagonise the other side.

On the other hand be aware that the party opposite may not have a genuine interest in settlement, and may only be there to assess the strengths and weaknesses of your case, using the mediation as a tactical device within the litigation (at whatever risk to himself on costs). If you suspect this to be the case do not duck the issue, and raise it with the mediator in caucus early on. Ask for some tangible sign of goodwill and consider whether your client's best interests are served by remaining if you are not reassured.

5.5 Private and Open Sessions

We have already discussed the flexibility with which the mediator can manage the process, and the range of meetings he has open to him, particularly in a multi-party or multi-level dispute. There he may have a plenary meeting and then joint or group sessions, and deal with experts or lawyers or laymen in parallel or sequential meetings. Do not be a passive observer on the question of management. Make a constructive contribution as to how you think your client's interests will be best served. You can and should disagree with the mediator if you have a good reason for doing so.

Open Sessions

Having both conducted and heard the presentations in the initial open or plenary session you will be in a position to consider the tactical advantages and disadvantages of such open sessions. Invariably the mediator will move into caucus sessions and rarely have another open session until settlement is achieved. He may utilise an open session to try and overcome a particularly difficult topic within the dispute where otherwise there is a complete logjam, the issue needs to be dealt with by the parties on a face to face basis, and the alternative is that one party or the other will leave. Occasionally either the advocate or the mediator may consider that conveying an explanation of a position or argument on a second hand basis will not be as effective as direct dialogue.

Try and gauge the impact of the first open meeting from its outset. Often it will be the first time a client and his advisers have met for a while; sometimes they may not previously have met at all; certainly it will be the first occasion on which the client and his own team have an opportunity to hear what the other side is saying first hand, and see how they are likely to appear in court. This will enable you to form a view about the value of the open sessions. If you are acting for a client who, by reason of his manner or appearance, age, sex or disability, or by virtue of the subject matter of the dispute, is someone that naturally attracts sympathy, make as much use of personal contact as possible. This restores the conflict to the level of personal ownership, and may make institutional opponents, or insurers standing behind them, very uncomfortable. It also provides a vulnerable or emotional client with a sense of having his or her 'day in court'.

Closed Sessions

The private or closed session, or caucus as it is sometimes called, is a central feature of the mediation process in the model most frequently used in Nigeria. One can do away with open meetings, including the joint opening session, and some mediators do; but in the civil/commercial model you cannot do without caucusing, since this is probably the most effective dynamic in mediation. Curiously the European and Harvard model, including that of the ICC, does not use caucusing and prefers the parties together all the time except for time-outs to seek advice.

In closed meetings the mediator holds a series of separate meetings with the parties in dispute. His aim is to bring the parties to a settlement by identifying hidden agendas and exploring problem solving proposals. The key is confidentiality. He will slowly build up trust, while at the same time offering the objective view of a neutral who is sympathetic to, but firm with, each party. But the mediator may only divulge what he has learned from one party in a closed session if express permission is given. You as the advocate must decide whether such permission should be given having first considered what, if any, impact such matters will have on the negotiation process. Sometimes the mediator will himself inform you that he would not advise disclosing a certain fact yet. On occasions he will hold the information ready to use when he thinks the time is right, which might be much later in the day, or may possibly remain unnecessary. There may be a conflict between you and your client about such disclosure, which should properly only be resolved in the absence of the mediator.

The caucus sessions are initially quite lengthy, particularly the first with each side, which is essentially an information-gathering exercise. These private meetings tend to speed up during the day, particularly once offers are made. Typically both parties will maintain in the initial open session and the early caucuses a legalistic position based on what they perceive as their rights (they remain in 'the Box' at Figure 1 p16). As time passes and confidence in both the process and the mediator grows, solutions that are based on the best interest of the parties rather than strictly perceived legal rights become acceptable.

There are various forms of separate or private meetings in which the mediator will have different objectives. He may wish to speak to the client alone without the advice, influence or pressure from that party's lawyer. Both you and your client should be prepared in advance to deal with such a proposal. Equally the mediator may wish to see all client parties together, but without their lawyers, to focus on commercial settlement options which might not necessarily reflect their strict legal interests. Or he may wish to see the lawyers for the opposing parties together without clients, to explore realistic settlement options where the parties are themselves proving intransigent, unrealistic in their expectations or problematic. In this case you must be particularly wary of inadvertent breaches of client confidentiality.

There are some common matters that should concern the advocate in dealing with private sessions:

- Irrespective of which type of private meeting you become involved in check the confidentiality position with the mediator at the end of each session.

- Avoid becoming, or letting the client become over anxious at the length of another party's separate meeting with the mediator.

- Be careful not to fall into the trap of misreading empathy by the mediator as a lack of neutrality.

- Try to use the mediator to obtain information from the other side that you may need to construct a settlement which may meet their needs.

- Do not get frustrated, or let the client get frustrated, by what appears to be a lack of progress during private sessions, particularly in the early stages of the appointment.

- Make the best use of periods following a private session with mediator to reflect on what has gone on during it to re-evaluate the case, your strategy, the options still open to your client, and to task the client appropriately.

5.6 The Role of the Advocate at the Mediation

Unlike the representative function of counsel at a trial, the mediation advocate is not present principally to convey his client's case to the mediator and the other side. He has an equally important role as his client's adviser. He must protect his client's best interests, as he sees them, while at the same time trying to make the process work. Occasionally these responsibilities conflict. The advocate must constantly evaluate the case and its progress in the mediation. He must stand up to an over-zealous mediator, when necessary. And while focusing on his client's legal interests, he must think laterally if a solution is to be found to overcome resistance while accommodating his client's legal position. To that extent the mediation advocate must release the client from the confines of the 'Box' (see Fig 1 at p16) and allow the mediator to investigate any wider agenda or needs, while at the same time using the legal case as a frame of reference with which to ascertain realistically the client's best and worst alternatives to a negotiated agreement.

Mediation is a team game. The client must be included in the process from start to finish. This extends to preparing together during mediation and taking advantage of quiet time outside caucus sessions to adjust negotiating strategy throughout. Thus, you should explain right through the day what is happening and why. This will help your client relax and approach negotiations constructively. His goals may change as information flows during the course of the mediation. You have to keep analysing the perceived strengths and weaknesses of your case, and of his approach to settlement, as the position changes.

Unsurprisingly, the lawyer will concentrate on issues of fact and law. The client, however, will have issues that may be of crucial importance to him but outside matters the lawyer sees as strictly relevant. When in joint session the advocate will usually either present the argument or support the decision-maker in presenting it. This will ensure that the joint meetings are concise, focussed on real issues, and there is less risk of the mediation coming to an abrupt halt if a party reacts unfavourably to misgivings or emotions. You should avoid up-beat submissions, but express your confidence in the merits balanced with an emphasis on attending the mediation in good faith and with the intention of finding a solution.

Advocacy during private sessions is equally different from trial work. A confrontational style is out of place. Consistent with defending your client's position, your mindset should be that the dispute is a problem to be solved not a conflict to be won. Therefore you need a constructive, problem solving approach, although the mediator must be persuaded of your points. You may need to overcome the mediator in caucus because he exerts a powerful influence. Allow him as a neutral to act instinctively. But be prepared to go back to the plenary session, to meet the lawyers on the other side, assist technical experts in a session confined to their discipline, and above all to view the process flexibly. This includes allowing discussions between clients and, where different, between principal decision-makers. For a lawyer to let go of his client in this way is difficult, but you must learn to let go at the right time.

You will need to support your client throughout the negotiation process: be a friend and supporter to the decision-maker when times get tough. This includes the position you should adopt outside sessions with the mediator or plenary sessions. This can be a rare and emotive situation for the lawyer, particularly if counsel is being instructed. Be active and use idle time creatively, advising on the strengths and weaknesses of both sides as they change. Consider inventive solutions as ways to overcome deadlock. Try to avoid entrenched positions; encourage your client to keep his temper under control, and as a last resort encourage him to stay when he talks of leaving.

The impact of your advocacy on the mediator, the other side and your own client, is likely to be dependent upon your preparation. It can be effective only if you are properly prepared and know your case throughout as much as for a trial, and you can analyse that of the other side for weaknesses. Without that knowledge it will be difficult to build a rapport with the client or provide good communication, and especially good listening. You also need to have an understanding as to why the client wants to take a certain course of action – his needs, motivations and desires. You will therefore have to cater for a non-legal approach, sometimes from the outset, and particularly where you have a weak case in law.

Know the documents. Even though there may only be a slim core bundle for the mediator, take all of your files. Know where to reach any document it transpires you must have, which the mediator has not seen. Often you may be required to answer a point raised by the other side and conveyed through the mediator.

Finally you will be required to draft the settlement agreement.[4] This will be invariably as soon as the parties have come to terms, although you may start parts of it beforehand. The parties may not reach agreement at the hearing but only a little while afterwards, prompted by the momentum built up on the day.

Objectives

You should have some objectives in mind prior to arriving at the session. This is, after all, the parties' day in court. It can be cathartic – an opportunity to divest the client of his problem on terms acceptable to both sides. Therefore it is too important an occasion to waste due to inadequate preparation, inability to negotiate or unwillingness to listen closely to the other side. An advocate will only be of benefit in the process if he understands that the basis of the conflict has now become an object of discussion rather than a partisan contest, as the parties try to educate the mediator what needs to be done to satisfy each side.

5.7 Working with the Mediator – Tactical Considerations

The mediator wishes to get a settlement. It is not his function to be an advocate, or to evaluate a position or advance what is fair. He is not concerned with whether the settlement is objectively fair, although it needs to satisfy both sides. Having said that, he is impartial, and must be trusted not to breach confidence. You must consider the issue of mutual trust and confidence between you and work at it to enable the mediator to do his job.

The mediator's training and technique is to get you to re-assess your client's position and risk, and to undermine your assessment of appropriate or effective settlement levels, and your client's expectation. He is likely to see you as resistant to the appropriate settlement level, at least at the outset of the mediation and perhaps for much of the day. As the day progresses he will look for the parties' underlying joint interests, and probe for the means to

---

[4] See p.130.

bring these closer and closer until, if possible, they overlap. This he will do by forcing each party to clarify its position. He keeps track of each party's changing stance; he directs the parties' attention from unproductive presentations, subtly analyses their line of reasoning and encourages them to broaden their perspective; he invents or helps new lines of progress towards workable solutions; he allows for the venting of emotional tensions and outbursts, and these he deflects or absorbs so as to encourage the parties to progress towards a settlement by generating an atmosphere of problem-solving enquiry. He will then have the lawyers assist him to draw together settlement options into a coherent package.

Although initially your client may regard the mediator as a quasi-judge and the process as some sort of quasi-trial, the advantages of the private session should dispel such notions. The client is here free from the stress of observation by the other side or by a judge. Both you and the mediator should promote the sense of privacy to make the client feel safe, and advance the dynamics of uninterrupted private communication. This is a three way process in which you have a relationship not only with your client but also with the mediator.

First, always be aware that the mediator will drive a wedge between you and your client if he thinks you are acting to impede a settlement. You should be able to overcome this if you are ready with innovative proposals, particularly those that add value to the process by solutions that are not available to a judge or arbitrator. You may work with the mediator to look for hidden agendas, and reveal the parties' true interests. If you have a difficult client you can use the mediator to deal with the situation known as reactive devaluation: this where your client will always place the worst interpretation on, or assume the worst intention of, an offer or statement coming from someone he regards as untrustworthy, whereas the same offer coming from someone seen as a friend or someone detached (i.e. the mediator) will either seem better or can at least be assessed more objectively. You should use the mediator to discuss proposals and options in front of your client, particularly where you yourself wonder whether the client is being frank with you or indeed himself about the real value of his position.

Although progress is driven by the ambit and momentum of the negotiations, you must remember that it is only the mediator who knows what both sides want. His aim will be to understand the parties' true interests and consequently obtain offers that overlap so that each party will obtain a settlement with which they are happy. This may not coincide with their strict legal rights, but if the client is in fact happy, do not let that concern you.

Throughout the hearing you should keep an eye on the mediator to ensure he is:

- including everyone in discussions;

- listening attentively to what has been said;

- demonstrating his understanding by responding and summarising; being neutral, open and non-judgmental;

- being approachable, open, friendly, and even-handed;

- observing and demonstrating confidentiality at all times.

5.8 Team Strategy

You must prepare and develop a settlement strategy, keeping the goal of mediation firmly in mind: you are there to settle, to stop the litigation costs clock running, and to stop your client's time being wasted by being engaged in the dispute, thus enabling him to get on with his business and his life. This means having an agenda that you may or may not want to disclose to the mediator. It may be in your client's interests to let the mediator know only part of his ambition, although generally as soon as you and your client feel confident in trusting the mediator he or she should be told all the client needs and wants. Among your client's agenda items will be those matters he wishes to prioritise: make sure you know what these are, and in due course, ensure the mediator is also aware of whatever is crucial. Work out with your client what he considers to be the value to him of each issue he wants to raise. Assess the realistic chances of success for each, bearing in mind that such an assessment is likely to change, and he will probably have to give way in a number of areas.

Work out how to apply your strategy according to the pace of the day. Negotiations usually start very slowly, with each side trying to justify its position to the mediator as a pre-cursor to making any offer; the tempo picks up as offers are finally exchanged and the settlement begins to crystallise, and then slows down at the end when difficult concessions have to be made – with the final arguments often being raised over minutiae. Applying your tactics to the pace of what is going on will enable you to assess when to offer more and when to stand firm, particularly in dealing with optimism bias, that is, the over optimistic forecast of the opposing lawyer and his client, and indeed, your own client. Know when to move, how far and in what direction.

In formulating your strategy for the day:

(i)   Determine the value of your client's settlement position in respect of each issue in dispute. Seek out those concessions that can be made at little cost.

(ii)   Identify new factors that might cause you to change your mind about the viability of your case e.g. new or clarified information; the capabilities of the other side now that you have seen them.

(iii) Develop a structured negotiation plan. Work out the point at which you will settle and how to get there.

(iv)   Avoid basing your offer or demand on the age of the case as it is being litigated or on its current position. The dynamics of mediation mean that cases settle much earlier than in litigation, often before statements of case and generally well before disclosure or the exchange of witness statements.

(v)   Plan to offer or demand at the mediation what your client eventually will or hopes to settle for. There is no point in holding back and hoping for a better outcome post-mediation.

(vi)   At the mediation don't see the mediator merely as a messenger, conveying offers with shuttle diplomacy. He or she will obtain information and use or re-frame it as they consider appropriate. Allow and expect him to have some leeway in developing possible outcomes.

(vii) Don't insist on monetary responses to your last offer. The mediator may get movement in principle in which each side tests offers without having to disclose, or yet disclose, a specific amount, for example 'we'll move if the other side moves'. You can test and make offers in general terms without having to disclose a specific amount.

(viii) Be candid with the mediator. Assist him to persuade the other side of the merits of your position, or how best to persuade them of it. He cannot act as a judge, but he can usefully identify and try to overcome misunderstandings and break down the problem of communication gaps leading to credibility issues, lack of trust between the parties and emotional or other grievances.

(ix)   Determine whether there are, and if so identify, any facts you do not want the mediator to disclose to your opponent. But bear in mind if you have facts which will affect the outcome of the contest, not much is to be gained by concealing them if the only difference is whether you settle now or later. There may be facts you do not want to tell the other side, but which may be helpful for the mediator to know in confidence.

(x)   Consider the position from the other side's perspective. How would your opposite number approach the debate?

(xi) Discuss your negotiating/settlement strategy with your client; tell him what you intend doing and why. Obtain regularly updated instructions on settlement during the course of the mediation when you are together privately.

(xii) Understand and apprehend the mediator's tactics, particularly how he will try to undermine your confidence in the strengths of your case even if he is a facilitative mediator.

A useful tool is to create a checklist for each stage of the negotiations. This will help clarify the current position and focus your thoughts on the next round:

1.   Where do negotiations stand now?

2.   Within what range will we settle?

3.   Do we need to adjust the range to accommodate what we now know?

4.   What do we need to learn from other side which will impact on that range?

5.   What offers/demands can we make to get within the range?

You should be conscious of the possibility of tension among your own party, for example between the ultimate decision maker and the person responsible for the dispute occurring. This may extend to friction between a principal and his representative – remember, agents have interests of their own which are rarely perfectly aligned with their client. A mediator may need to exploit this tension if he can identify it, and you will need a defensive strategy when that occurs.

Do not worry about being seen to be co-operative. A conciliatory approach does not mean folding. Your task is to conduct a principled and structured negotiation. Your client will appreciate progress more than your robustness. The mediator will appreciate assistance in reaching his goal, although assisting the mediator does not extend to abandoning the client. You must protect him, for example by the use of adjournments if your client is flagging or becoming drained.

Your tactics may in fact be dictated by express instructions from your client or his insurers. Some claims managers now have considerable experience of mediation and feel that they can exploit the process by being tough negotiators. For example they may make offers only open for acceptance on the day of the mediation or prejudicial information might be produced which has not been seen before, or a defendant's insurer may simply refuse to increase an offer. You need to be in a position to deal with such scenarios, to protect your client as necessary from such pressure and to ensure that his confidence is sustained.

5.9 Working towards a Settlement

Perhaps the most difficult notion for the lawyer acting as a mediation advocate to grasp is that he does not need to obtain a legal solution to the problem. It is not necessary to build the settlement around rights and liabilities, just needs and interests. Rights and liabilities are only relevant in terms of projecting the likely outcome of a trial for the purpose of applying pressure to settle. The underlying interests may have nothing to do with rights or liabilities. If the mediator can expose these interests, practical and creative solutions may be available, at least as options. That is why lateral and creative thinking are so important to the process.

You must know your client's BATNA (best alternative to a negotiated agreement) and how to improve on it if possible. Equally you must know the WATNA (worst alternative to a negotiated agreement) and ensure that this includes costs and interest. But more than this, you should anticipate the other side's equivalent position. "The more you can learn of their options the better prepared you are for negotiation. Knowing their alternatives, you can realistically estimate what you can expect from the negotiation. If they appear to over estimate their BATNA, you will want to lower their expectations."[5]

Be curious about your opponent's position. Try to find the breakthrough or 'tipping point', which will cause movement and generate a sufficient momentum to bring about the settlement. You need to achieve a deal that

---

[5] Fisher R., and Ury W, *Getting to Yes: Negotiating an Agreement Without Giving In* Penguin 2003 p.109.

suits everyone, since that is the desired outcome without which your client will not be able to get anything he wants: there is a balance to be struck between protecting your client's own interests by declining to offer concessions and failing to get any advantageous agreement at all.

You also need to discover what the client really wants. You have to be as much aware as the mediator of the difference between positions and interests, demands and needs, and claims and motivations.

5.10 Effective Mediation Management

The single most common reason for a dispute going to trial is that the client refuses to accept a reasonable offer of settlement, recommended as such by his own lawyer. Occasionally there are no offers made, but this is becoming increasingly unusual where parties are obliged to protect their position at the earliest possible stage in the proceedings against the possibility that a trial judge may disallow costs where parties have not shown sufficient enthusiasm for ADR. The refusal to accept reasonable offers would suggest that lawyers need to keep in better communication with their clients about the true nature, risks and cost of litigation, the possibilities of settlement as a solution, and of all the important developments in the case.[6] If this is true of litigation, it is certainly true of mediation.

A study of personal injury litigation in New York in the 1970s[7] concluded that the more actively involved the client, the better the outcome for that client. The mediation advocate can thus better serve his client by keeping him actively engaged in the process. There are a number of strategies for this that can best be effected during the day in the privacy of the caucus room when the mediator is not present. These include:

(a)   At the outset, before the opening plenary session, make clear if you have not already done so, or otherwise repeat the basic procedure to be expected during the day. Explain the probability that the dispute can be resolved by negotiation, rehearse the difficulties with litigation and discuss the kind of problems likely to be encountered. Make sure the client understands that he has a right to reject actions that both you and the mediator may recommend. Also get the client to confirm that the

---

[6] See Williams, Gerald R., *Lawyers as Healers and Warriors* CEDR Seminar Papers September 1997 p.54.
[7] Rosenthal, D.E. *Lawyer and Client: Who's in Charge?* Russell Sage Foundation 1974.

settlement being negotiated will compromise the whole of the present claim or dispute, and where specified, all disputes between the parties.

(b)   Discuss with your client how his actions during the day might affect the negotiations. Advise him how he can help you. Caution him, if necessary, about his approach to the other side; conversely make sure he understands that he can say what he likes and express how he feels about the situation. You may in effect have to counsel him in areas relating to the claim, be they emotional, financial, or referable to his family, employment or health.

(c)   Keep him informed throughout the day of how you see the mediation progressing. This will enable you to receive instant feedback from your client, and enable you to fine tune your strategy.

(d)   Make sure he is informed about the relevant choices that are open to him at any one time. Identify what alternatives are available, and provide him with your professional experience in dealing with each alternative and their anticipate difficulties and benefits. If there are occasions, which require the client to provide informed consent to what you propose as the advocate, confirm his understanding of the position as the last task before resuming negotiations or seeing the mediator.

5.11 Negotiation Processes and Strategies within Mediation

Always be aware that ADR is concerned with the appropriateness to the client of the dispute resolution – you are meeting the client's best needs for resolving his dispute. Contrast this with litigation, where most of the court process is designed to compensate harm with an award of money. That is a pernicious doctrine because in many cases money is only a poor substitute for the loss suffered,[8] particularly a physical or psychological injury.

Do not think that, while important, money is everything. The process of negotiation is not simply a process of bargaining where you are haggling to

---

[8] The themes in this section and 5.14 to 5.20 are developed from the investigatory work of Professor Gerald R. Williams, J Reuben Clark Law School, Brigham Young University, Utah, USA drawn from his Materials on Negotiation and Conflict Resolution for Lawyers used in the CEDR seminar *'Are You a Co-operative or Aggressive Negotiator and Does it Matter? Lawyers as Healers and Warriors*. September 1997 afterwards referred to as 'Williams'.

get nearer to your side of the middle of a monetary amount. It will enable you to evaluate the potential for joint gains and discover the interests and needs of *both* sides, including money but not exhaustively. Negotiation is interaction with a goal in mind.

Mediators recognise that, fortunately, lawyers are reasonably predictable due to their common training and shared or similar experiences in practice – they are basically co-operative since the professions lay great store in the concept of fraternity. Lawyers and other professionals perform and develop their positions over the duration of the mediation using information skills, and the process of lawyerly negotiation is structured with generally, a clear beginning, a middle and an end. The advocates know there must be movement in order to compromise. They focus on when, why and how.

Competent and effective negotiation must be the subject of adequate preparation. For the purpose of preparing this stage of the mediation:

- You must feel ready, otherwise do not negotiate.

- Your factual preparation must involve the client – this will provide him with a better understanding of the true nature of the case.

- Decide what your objectives are: money, or money plus other joint interests.

- You should have a clear strategy as to how you will reach your goals.

- Try to keep part of the process task orientated: make the other side work to prove their negotiating position by demonstrating where the numbers come from.

- Devise questions for the other side that can only be answered by the client, not his lawyer, to draw the opposite party directly into the process.

- Make sure you can bring your own client to settlement – if you have any doubt about this you must be prepared to negotiate with your own client.

Most people are conflict avoiders – they will absorb the harm done to them in order to get on with their lives – or at least they are conflict neutral. They are pushed into conflict by a straw that breaks the camel's back. They ascribe blame to the person or entity they perceive is doing them harm, and raise a claim. They need an avenue through which to channel conflict when their claim is rejected. That avenue leads to negotiation, mediation, arbitration and trial.[9] Mediation is assisted or managed negotiation. But in spite of its flexibility and its advantages over an arbitral system, mediation cannot escape from the necessary rituals embodied in negotiation.

First you must understand the difference between positional and principled negotiation. In litigation the lawyer who has to negotiate will generally engage in positional bargaining or haggling. Here each side takes up a position based on the outcome needed. The negotiator will focus on why he needs a particular outcome and what he can offer in return or demand as part of the process. He will haggle, threaten, or swap concessions and usually agree somewhere in the middle of the bargaining range. The difficulty with positional bargaining is that to improve the outcome, generally by extending the bargaining range at one end so as to accommodate a movement nearer your position than half way, subject to professional ethics, there is an incentive to misrepresent the position or your client's interests, to withhold sensitive information, make threats, bluff, dig your heels in or wait unreasonably, fail to listen to the other side, make only small and low concessions, make no concession without getting a return, and, occasionally, use walking out as a tactic. This approach is likely to produce only a limited outcome, and one that might give rise to future problems if there is an ongoing relationship.

Principled bargaining is a problem solving method in which you aim for a wise outcome produced in an efficient and amicable way, by negotiating on merits not merely advancing claims. Mediators are taught to work 'hard on the problem, soft on the people', to use objective criteria, to separate the personality issues from the problem, to focus on interests and invent options for mutual gain. Mediators therefore tend to move positional bargaining into principled bargaining. The dynamic works because the mediator has no stake in the dispute – a party is therefore less likely to adopt a positional negotiating stance with the mediator and is therefore more likely to reveal his real objectives and what he is prepared to concede.

The mediator introduces the element of 'objective criteria' into the parties' understanding of their own position. He can, if asked and he agrees, give an outside view on the validity of the case or the fairness of a proposal. He will exploit the differences between parties' perceptions of risk. He will seek to

---

[9] Burgess, John *Mediation Skills: What the Mediator Wants from Advocates* 1 Serjeants Inn February 2005.

build up momentum towards a settlement by obtaining movement on a number of easy items. He may suggest non-party assistance in resolving difficult issues, by asking for further information, or provide tasks for the parties on each side to perform, such as number crunching. He will look for productive trade-offs, for example by suggesting that if the other side are willing to move on this, you should move on that.

The mediator will break up the formality or rhythm of the day if he thinks it will help. He may defer certain issues. He will certainly be a constructive force: he will emphasise positive progress and diffuse language with emotional content by channelling hostility between the parties into solving problems. An important role is to help parties save face in moving from previous strongly held positions.

Although the opening plenary session is intended normally only to establish your client's current position it may turn into an open preliminary negotiating session, or subsequently you may find yourself in open negotiation. Persuasion at a joint meeting will require a balance between empathy and assertiveness – be neither aggressive nor submissive: assume your client's interests are legitimate and valid; explain to the other side in the presence of the mediator your own interests, needs and perspectives. Express an understanding of your opponent's argument, or at least a desire to understand. Be neither overtly sympathetic nor indicate agreement, but listen attentively and actively, looking for areas of potential mutual gain. Try, if you can, to lay the foundation for problem solving – at the outset find a framework within which to negotiate as part of a reciprocal process that will allow both parties to emphasise their case and make the necessary assertions while at the same time avoid position-taking by identifying interests, needs, resources and capabilities. Do not evaluate what is said until later in private session. Try to brainstorm suggestions as a problem solving exercise, but without asserting ownership of any ideas that may be produced, and keep your client's ambitions realistic.

There are particular stresses to be encountered in open negotiating sessions, particularly where you are having to cope with running instructions, evaluate offers, look for potential problems, and understand and explain the risks to your client. The following guidance should be of practical assistance:

- Do not agree if you disagree.

- Always check with the client before making a concession.

- Explain the story – make sure the other side understands what you are saying.

- Make sure your client understands what the other side is saying.

- Establish within the specific context of the present negotiation what is important to your client, and why, and also establish whether there is anything else which is important to him.

- Do not lose any momentum - move on to the next objective once you have achieved all that you think you can achieve.

- Try to evaluate what is going on at all times – do not be confused by the negotiation dynamic.

- Be aware of the allocation of risk between the parties in any proposed solution to the dispute which is more creative than an award of money.

- Be aware of the allocation of risk between the parties should the mediation fail: at the point at which you stand, who will lose out more if one party decides to walk out?

- Look at the longer term.

- Anticipate problems.

- Don't take everything that is being said at face value. Read between the lines and try to decode messages.

It is far easier to negotiate in mediation if there are two or more issues to be resolved. If that is the case, negotiations involve integrating the interests of the parties. Where such interests may dovetail, there is genuine potential for joint gains, value can be created for both sides, and the 'pie' can be expanded before it is divided. By having subsidiary issues which can be resolved either by making concessions or giving away assets without injury to your client, you may be able to avoid inflicting needless harm on the opposing party and find it much easier getting to 'yes'. If, on the other hand, there is only a single issue being contested, there is only a limited distribution available, and aggressive negotiators tend to win. If there is no potential for joint gains it is difficult to argue for anything except to claim value for your own side and try to destroy the other's expectation or its investment in its own case. Therefore even single issue disputes should be deconstructed to look for potential mutual gains.

5.12 The Momentum to Expect

For the mediator the appointment will run in a series of phases with which he is familiar: introductory, information gathering, identifying solutions and problem solving, negotiation and bargaining, and settlement. The client's approach to the dynamics of negotiation in a successful mediation tends to pass through five different kinds of common stages or steps, all well known to behavioural psychologists:

(I) Denial

Your client will maintain he is not at fault, or he is not the one who needs to change. He has no conscious knowledge of the needs or desires of others, and no particular interest in meeting them unless they coincide with his own interests.

(II) Acceptance

He concedes that he may be part of the problem. This is a painful transition for the client. He moves to a position where he can accept that even if he is not part of the problem he may be able to find or move towards the solution.[10]

(III) Sacrifice

This stage is concerned with realisation and letting go. First comes a realisation by your client that there are two sides to the story in question, and the other side may have legitimate reasons for being so upset, or defensive, or vindictive; or worse, the possibility he might not win or those opposite not lose. Having moved from his original position there is something of a ritual mortification: he will have to sacrifice his pride, or greed, envy, arrogance, vanity, or conceit, and the belief in his own infallibility, his unwillingness to acknowledge another's point of view or needs, or his unwillingness to forgive another. It is at this point that the client is at his most vulnerable, although any cathartic experience will also commence here.

(IV) Leap of Faith

Mediation is powerful because it facilitates leaps of faith in a way that litigation cannot. Even agreeing to mediation is a leap of faith since your client may worry that this alone may be perceived by the other side as a sign

---

[10] Williams p.44; Williams, Gerald R. *A Lawyer's Handbook for Effective Negotiation and Settlement* 5th ed. West 1995.

of weakness. That said, once your client recognises that winning is no longer a foregone conclusion, and that movement must come from him, using the mediator reduces the risk involved in leaps of faith. The progress towards settlement starts with small mutually reciprocal steps, apology, an acknowledgement of wrong doing or wrong thinking, or concessions about the nature of his behaviour. This is answered by forgiveness, and that replied to with contrition. Once the emotion has been broken with a leap of faith, negotiations to create a practical solution can follow.

(V) Renewal/Reconciliation

The final dynamic in the process is one of coming together, the healing of relations, or at least those positive feelings engendered by having reached a concluded agreement. Even if a fractured relationship is difficult to mend, the relief in having finalised the dispute gives a sense of renewal.

5.13 Traits of Effective and Ineffective Negotiators

Since the 1970s American academics have been studying the profiles of experienced negotiators,[11] categorising them broadly as 'co-operative' or 'aggressive' and attempting to establish whether those bearing such profiles were effective, ineffective or average negotiators. The results of such research have concluded that up to 87% of negotiators performed more effectively when they were co-operative. Of those who considered themselves aggressive negotiators (20% of the numbers studied) 85% were found to be ineffective or average in terms of results achieved, and only 15% effective. This suggests that the aggressive negotiator is likely to achieve the result he wishes in less than one in every six mediations in which he is the advocate. That is a sobering thought for those of you who believe that negotiation is about projecting strength in order to overcome your opponent. For every time such tactics work, there will most likely be five when they do not.

Professor Gerald Williams of Brigham Young University, Utah, USA analysed the objectives and traits of effective and ineffective negotiators in the following way.[12]

> "The effective cooperative negotiator is the embodiment of the idea of creating a win/win situation in which both sides get a fair settlement, while getting the best settlement available for his client.

---

[11] Williams p.28, 29.
[12] Williams p.30-32.

His conduct is trustworthy, ethical and fair; in negotiation he will be courteous, personable, tactful, sincere and fair-minded. He presents a realistic opening position, accurately evaluates the case and, in relative terms, does not make threats. He will engage in movement co-operatively (sometimes this is known as cooperative thrusts), but will use the strategy of tit-for-tat[13] both to protect his client's standpoint, probe his opponent's position and to secure the most gains available. He is willing to share information since cooperatives solve problems by reference to the merits rather than by shying away from their difficulties. He uses understatement and assumes that truth will out and speak for itself. The problem is that he is vulnerable to the aggressive negotiator who has no bounds of fairness, who will push him back if he can, and who assumes that if you back up you have no holding ground.

The effective aggressive negotiator has a zest for the well-fought contest. Although he wants to maximise the settlement for his client, he is unconcerned about establishing a win/win situation if he can win on a win/ lose situation, and if by outdoing or outmanoeuvring his opponent, he can be seen to be the winner. He is dominant, forceful and attacking; well prepared and uncooperative, he is a very good strategist and tactician who plans the timing and sequence of events and applies these rigidly. He will get to know his opponent but be entirely disinterested in the other side's needs. In his general approach there is a danger of overkill: he will usually begin with an unrealistic opening position; he will use threats freely in an attempt to intimidate; he reveals information only gradually, as if he was engaged in a game of deception, and he is willing to stretch the facts.

Both cooperative and aggressive negotiators who are effective share certain traits. They are equally well prepared, realistic, self-controlled, convincing, perceptive at reading clues, and well versed in applying legal skills. In contrast both cooperative and aggressive negotiators may be ineffective due to certain traits.

The ineffective cooperative negotiator wants to maintain good relations with his opponent in order to get a deal that will meet his client's needs. This makes him obliging, patient and forgiving. He projects an image of being honest and trustful which may border on the gullible or naïve. He will be pressed to give away more and more without securing any advantage in return. His will is overborne since

---

[13] See p.125.

he feels the need to be nice to his opponent even when a normal person should be more aggressive. It is one thing to be obliging, but a successful negotiator needs to have the strength of will to be otherwise, and if he makes concessions, this should only be on the basis of a conscious choice.

The ineffective aggressive negotiator has some undesirable traits that make him fail. He is overtly hostile, arrogant, obnoxious and irritating. He is in fact unprepared on the facts and the law and he tends to bluff. He uses aggression as a substitute for preparation. In face-to-face negotiation he is quarrelsome, demanding and argumentative, often using a take-it-or-leave it approach. He is intolerant of and hostile to the needs of others, and his bullying approach leads the negotiations to collapse since he will inevitably drive the other side away from the negotiating table unless it is in an extremely weak position."

To an extent the lay client will expect his advocate to adopt the techniques of both the effective cooperative and aggressive negotiator as he sees the day progress. The experienced mediation advocate will understand that he is engaged in a ritual process and be patient with it, tolerating a less mature opponent. He will be vigilant and perceptive, allowing himself temporarily to suspend judgment, contain and channel energy, endure criticism, think quickly and act decisively.

5.14 Ten Rules for Effective Negotiation[14] within Mediation

1. Do not demand an outcome that is not fair to both sides

You want an outcome that is fair to your own client, and are unlikely to agree to anything less. But there is little to be gained from pushing your opponent to accept an outcome that his client will be unhappy with. If it is positively harmful to one party that is only creating a problem for the future.

2. Give continuous feedback to the other side, immediately if possible

Keeping up the momentum is all-important in negotiation. Indicating agreement, disagreement or re-emphasising and explaining your own position can best achieve this. But it is essential to keep dialogue going. If

---

[14] Developed from Williams pp 62-5.

you can, express positive agreement that takes issues out of consideration and promotes a feeling of progress, although there will be some circumstances where you should not appear to be too eager. Expressing disagreement is also imperative: do not let the other side build up its expectations without knowing you have a problem with a proposal – give negative feedback immediately, but be tactful and empathetic – and do not silently accept things that hurt your position. You can show that you are willing to be persuaded to change your mind and will make your concession at the appropriate time.

3. Maintain your factual position every time it is challenged

Both your opponent and the mediator will challenge your factual, and possibly your legal, position probing for weaknesses and uncertainties with the intention of undermining your commitment to your client's case. Re-emphasise your points every time they are challenged. Add new information where necessary, or restate the existing information in different ways, but do not let a challenge pass without comment.

4. Observe body language

In any open session look closely at your opponent and his client. Become conscious of the strength of conviction in what they are saying by observing their use of body language. Remember that you will also be making signals, consciously or otherwise. Be conscious of your own body language and what messages you may be sending – some mediators are trained in assessing non-verbal communication.

5. Use your team as observers

You cannot hope to see everything, particularly if you are immersed in advocacy. Use other members of your team – client, solicitor, insurer, expert or other witness – as observers, and question them as to how they perceive any open-session negotiations to be going. Let them either reinforce or contradict your own view. Do not waste the fact of their being present.

6. Be a contrarian

When in private play devil's advocate. Put yourself in your opponent's shoes and try to ascertain what tactics he must use to achieve his aims. This will not only enable you to see what should be coming, but also help you dispel misunderstanding or mistrust if you want to be a cooperative negotiator.

7. Convey an impression of professionalism, integrity, confidence and efficiency

It goes almost without saying that a good impression will carry you forward, and a bad one will hamper your efforts from the outset.

8. Look appropriately prepared

Visual impression, though worthy, is not enough. Have your law, facts, calculations and options ready for presentation. Never proceed until you are ready, since to do so will always work against your client's interests. Asking for more time should never prejudice you.

9. Sustain a clear, distinct factual and legal theme throughout the negotiation

Nothing is more persuasive than a clear theme supported by factual and legal points. It does not need to be complex nor the solutions offered complicated, but it should be organised and presented with confidence.

10. Minimise your reliance upon notes

Know what you are going to say, whether to the mediator or to your opponent. Have your facts and argument ready so that you can concentrate on the other person, not your notes, during the negotiation. Constantly referring to notes makes you look unprepared, less confident of your case, and less sure of yourself. This should not stop you making notes when in negotiation, although this is a distraction which should be used sparingly. Make sure you understand what is being said before you write it down.

5.15 Negotiating Phases[15]

Just as psychologists have identified well-defined stages in the mediation process, so researchers have observed that most negotiation develops through certain phases. At the beginning negotiators establish a working relationship and adopt respectively their initial bargaining positions. Aggressive negotiators will try to convey the impression that they are irrevocably committed to their opening position. This, the opening phase of the negotiation, is actually quite lengthy with no perceptible movement by either side.

---

[15] See Williams, Gerald R: *A Lawyer's Handbook for Effective Negotiation and Settlement* 5th edn West 1995.

The middle stage of a negotiation commences when some outside factor gives impetus to the process, usually some sort of time deadline. At that point the negotiators commence working seriously on the question of whether an agreement is possible. This is when alternative solutions, compromise and concession making are sought.

The final stage is the most crucial. As the deadline approaches a crisis is often reached: the negotiators often feel trapped by the choice of whether to accept the last offer or let the mediation fail, unless another alternative can be devised. As a process either agreement is reached or the parties declare an impasse. If there is a settlement the parties will work out the details of the agreement; if an impasse is declared, the parties will have to make alternative arrangements, such us furthering the claim in litigation.

5.16 Opening Negotiating Positions

In negotiating psychology the first number is the most potent number in the negotiations since it must influence the second number. It must be selected with great care, balancing the fear that you cannot get what you don't ask for, with being so aggressive that the other side want to leave immediately. You must consider the likely impact on the other side of adopting a maximalist position, which is where you ask for considerably more than you expect to obtain by making a very high opening demand.

Contrast this with actually opening by asking for what you feel is fair to both sides (the 'equitable position'), either by giving your anticipated bottom line straight away, or by inflating your demand by a 'reasonable' amount which you will afterwards concede. A party that opens with his true bottom line has no room for manoeuvre except by offering alternative or additional non-monetary solutions.

Whether you start with a maximalist or equitable opening, the effective mediation negotiator will explore a variety of alternative solutions to the dispute in the hope of arriving at an optimum solution which provides the greatest possible benefit and the least possible damage to both sides, often looking at something the other side haven't considered.

Both sides may safely assume that the opening position is a product of posturing, and that both sides will be willing to move in order to obtain a settlement. The suggestion that one side or the other is unalterably committed to its opening position is illusory, although it may take a significant amount of time for the illusion to be dispelled since it will have been supported by reference to the legal and factual elements of the case.

5.17 Movement

The first impediment to securing movement in the negotiations is overcoming bluff and getting the other side to enter seriously into dialogue. It is a convention among lawyers to pretend that the lawyer who first suggests settlement has the weaker case; by the same token many lawyers believe that by holding out against settlement discussions they imply that theirs will be a winning case at trial. This is particularly true of insurer defendants and defence lawyers, for whom delay is normally advantageous. Both of these beliefs have led to cases proceeding to trial only to settle hurriedly at the last moment.

By electing to go to mediation, or having been nudged in that direction by the court, you have the benefit of the same context for negotiation, but the absence of pressure will pervade the opening part of the day unless there is strong independent motivation for the parties to start coming together. Movement comes only as the day wears on and it is apparent that there will be no point to the mediation without it: one party or the other will be asked by the mediator to put up or shut up – he will press both sides to say in clear terms whether they are here to obtain a settlement or not. At that point your predetermined scheme for subtly reducing your opening position should come into effect, either as the prime mover or in reply to a hint of movement from the other side. At the outset it need not be explicit or even a formulated cash offer, and can be based on principle – 'if you move, so will we'. Eventually the degrees of movement will crystallise into firm offers which usually also conform to a recognised pattern. This involves initially small movement followed by fairly large-scale movement, and then finally, very small-scale movement as you tentatively approach settlement. Invariably the last steps are the hardest.

5.18 Crisis and Deadlock

The point of crisis comes with the arrival of a deadline, and this can give rise to intense psychological pressure. Both a strong opponent and the mediator will use it. You may be faced with what you perceive to be the final offer from the other side; or the mediator may be relying upon a 'locked-door' syndrome to achieve a breakthrough. The pressure comes with the realisation by your party that should the last offer be refused the mediation will fail, and further litigation costs will be expended, and the trial perceived as inevitable; alternatively if the last offer is accepted your client will never know if you could have achieved more or paid less.

The way to break this psychological pressure is to remember that you are in fact not caught in a yes/no situation. The client always has three choices: (i) to accept your opponent's last offer, (ii) to reject your opponent's last offer, walk away and go to trial, or (iii) to come up with a new proposal. It is the third choice that is often the key to success. This third option prevents unnecessary deadlock, keeps the negotiation alive and puts pressure on your opponent to accept your revised offer. The closer you are to the deadline, the more seriously your opponent must consider your offer. Therefore always be in a position to modify your last offer as the best way to save face at the moment of deadlock, keep the process going and deflect the pressure of the crisis point to the other side.

Remember that the deadline may not be uniform and for reasons unknown to you the other side may have an entirely different time limit of their own. Deadlines can relate to the litigation, for example the imminence of the trial, the next case management conference or court direction, after the lifting of any automatic stay pending dispute resolution, or they can be fact related, for example the next delivery or payment due, the application of pressure from the bank on your client's credit, the next tranche of legal fees due, or pressure coming from other sources. The pre-arranged end of the mediation session is also a deadline that creates strong psychological pressure, although this is usually artificial since if the parties wish to continue and the mediator considers it worthwhile, either the mediation or bi-partisan negotiations can continue by agreement. If you or your client has a particular personal deadline – catching the last train, or flying out – it is unwise to reveal this as your opponent may use such a difficulty as a pressure point, even if he is the most cooperative of negotiators.

5.19 Dealing with Obnoxious Opponents[16]

What do you do when faced with an opponent who is irritating, rigid, hostile, arrogant, quarrelsome and egotistical? We have all come across professionals who serve their egos, not their clients, and who create a situation that is frustrating and considerably impedes the progress of the day.

---

[16] This and the following passage draw heavily from Williams's *Solving Particular Problems In Legal Negotiation* pp57-61.

How do you negotiate with such a person? The key is self-control. You must not give way to your basic impulse to fight fire with fire – if you lose your own patience and goodwill the negotiations will be over before they start and your side will leave the mediation with a strong sense of wasted time and costs, which you may blame on the process itself. The fighting fire with fire approach will almost certainly lead to deadlock and failure.

Your aim is to outwit such negotiators by calling their bluff, putting maximum pressure on them to change their tactics and deal with you on a realistic and rational level. To do so you need to exercise enormous restraint to prevail successfully against an irritating opponent. Keep your temper. Don't quarrel. Give him a soft answer (at the risk of maddening him).

Remember that an opponent acting in this way is often unprepared on the facts and the law, unsure of the true value of his case and is therefore using bluff and bluster as a substitute. Adopt a position that you will not negotiate with this person so long as the irritating tactics continue: do not initiate negotiations while they do, and do not accede to your opponent's attempts to negotiate. Keep occasional or even frequent contact to educate him about the case, refer him to key facts and documents, or indicate key developments on your side. Make your communications non-threatening and invite co-operation. Express empathy and openly promise that you will commence your negotiation when the time is right. But all the time refuse to negotiate so long as the irritating tactics continue. Indicate your preparedness for the litigation to go on.

Be patient. Remember that if he is ineffective as a negotiator he is likely to be equally ineffective at trial. He should fold and either accept an invitation to negotiate on a reasonable and rational basis, or, if he chooses to have his side abandon the mediation, a wedge will usually have been driven between him and his client's confidence in his ability. You may well be negotiating with someone else shortly afterwards, with whom you can achieve a pre-trial settlement.

5.20 Dealing with Overly Aggressive Opponents

When facing an effective aggressive opponent it is well to understand four basic defensive principles:[17]

---

[17] Four basic principles of verbal self defence - Elgin, Suzette Haden *The Gentle Art of Verbal Self-Defense* Prentice-Hall 1980 pp 3-5 Williams 58-61.

(i)   Know you are under attack.

(ii)   Know what kind of attack you're facing. Learn to judge and recognise your opponent's weapons, his strength and his level of skill.

(iii)   Know how to make your defence fit the attack – the response must match each aggressive move, it must be an appropriate response and at an appropriate level of intensity – proportionate and sufficient to secure your aim.[18]

(iv)   Know how to follow through – you must be able to carry out your response once you have chosen it. Be prepared to feel and work through a certain amount of guilt, since healthy people don't enjoy causing other people pain even when it is well and thoroughly deserved.

When attempting to defuse the potency of an aggressive opponent, as a cooperative negotiator you will need to:

- Deal more effectively with the facts: accept the burden of demonstrating the credibility of your own facts. Prove you have something worth paying for. Recognise that your aggressive opponent will skilfully seek to discredit your facts. He and his client will have set their expectations by how far you are willing to let them go. Stay with your facts until your opponent recognises that there are strong points in your case and understands what they are.

- Present facts serially, not all together. Look for the reaction of your opponent on an item-by-item basis and decide what to do by reading their reaction.

- Present facts in their strategically most favourable light.

- Recognise that parties inevitably have a different view of the facts. Do not try to persuade your opponent to adopt your view of the facts, rather to take your view of them into account.

- Express willingness to change your view if he can demonstrate his position convincingly.

---

[18] See Tit-for-tat p.125.

- Repeat the facts as often as they are challenged. Often the aggressive negotiator's strategy is to ignore or refute your facts. The solution is to show that your facts can sustain his attack.

- Adopt opening positions favourable to your client but clearly communicate that the position is temporary since the parties' interests and needs are not yet fully known, that some facts require more careful consideration, and that you invite and seek a creative solution for joint gains.

- Make few unilateral concessions, and never make a unilateral concession on the merits. Use the requirement of your client's approval as device to stall on concessions. Make only concessions that do not hurt your position. Withhold any major concessions until a suitable package can be put together – make it at least a two-stage process. In order to preserve the negotiating climate you can acknowledge the other sides' interests and needs, and indicate that concessions will be made, but explain with good reasons why they are not available at present.

- Respond immediately and unambiguously to aggressive moves. Avoid mirroring aggressive behaviour but use a counter move: require an explanation, or a reference to the facts; cushion your response with empathy; express a recognition that a different point of view might be valid; admit your source of information may be wrong; use the need for consultation and instructions as a buffer, but never flatly refuse – give reasons, and consistently decline to make unwise or premature concessions; elaborate factors which weigh against granting requests, keep your client's options open, leave room to manoeuvre, and, like a proverbial boy scout, be prepared and look prepared.

When dealing with this kind of an opponent refuse to 'play the same game.' Disarm him by asking 'why' frequently – seek explanations for demands being made – and have him identify what are the interests sought to be met by the demands he is making. Look for objective criteria. And try to shame him – question his sense of fairness and whether his client really wants a settlement.

5.21 Using Tit-For-Tat as a Model Negotiating Strategy

There is a useful method for creating a balance between cooperative and aggressive negotiation, devised for use in game theory and usually referred to as the Anatole Rappaport model *'the Prisoner's Dilemma'*.[19] It is the simple but effective strategy known as tit-for-tat, and it is this: always begin cooperatively then respond tit-for-tat to each cooperative or aggressive move by the other side.

As a tactical device it has six qualities that make it useful when negotiating in mediations:

1. It begins cooperatively, although cooperation is based on both anticipation of and the fact that cooperation will be mutual.

2. It retaliates perfectly in the sense that the response will be immediate, unambiguous, and appropriate – the cooperative negotiator will be vigilant of attack and will react, making it clear he is acting responsively to unacceptable aggression from the other side.

3. It is perfectly trustworthy – the negotiator never moves aggressively unless he is attacked.

4. It forgives perfectly – the response is immediate, unambiguous, and appropriate.

5. It is not greedy – the response doesn't object to gains made by other side because they should be mutual.

6. It is perfectly patient: as a device it doesn't try to shortcut the negotiation process – it follows the ritual of negotiation.

Useful as tit-for-tat is in negotiation it does have one flaw of which to be wary: if one side mis-reads the other by interpreting a non-aggressive move as an attack, the misreading side will retaliate. The innocent side will respond in kind with both continuing to believe the other side started it. Such a situation can only be broken by a leap of faith by a cooperative negotiator, or by tracing the problem back to its source.

---

[19] See Allman, William F *Nice Guys Finish First* Science (1984) vol 5 no 8 p25-31; Axelrod, Robert *The Evolution of Cooperation* Basic Books 1984.

5.22 Forensic Skills of Mediation Advocates

Dealing With The Client

- Be with the client physically and psychologically.

- Make him feel trustful and important by your display of interest.

- Do not interrupt him; do not ask him too many questions.

- Do not summarise what he is saying; acknowledge and empathise.

- Do not finish his sentences; don't use clichés in the way you speak to him, or be judgmental.

- Do not criticise his behaviour.

- If you need to question him use open questions, rather than cross examine him or asking rhetorical questions.

- Once you have concluded a settlement, take the time and effort needed to justify and support the agreement: your client needs to feel happy about it so that he will not subsequently want to renounce or challenge it.

Dealing with the Mediator

- Avoid extreme opening offers and incremental concessions.

- He is likely to be able to see through artificial tactics – stonewalling, threatening, becoming angry, intimidating, ridiculing, or indeed, lying. In particular try not to lie to the mediator. Although he is not a judge and the mediation is not a court setting, it is not very becoming conduct or attractive in a lawyer or a professional man, and it is usually unproductive and potentially very damaging to the settlement dynamics if discovered by either mediator or the other side. It will lead to an immediate loss of the trust and confidence necessary to provide the momentum towards settlement; it might be impossible to recover.

- Be courteous.

- Do not talk over the mediator or your client or demonstrably fail to listen.

- Do not fake paying attention.

- Do not fail to disclose helpful information.

- Do not fix upon a single solution or run to the bottom line too quickly.

- Do not make allegations in bad faith as a negotiating tool, or fail to prioritise the client's needs.

- Do not assume the mediator will communicate with the other side as directed by you or your client – merely because he is given permission to carry some piece of information or even offer to the other side do not assume that he will do so, either when asked or at all.

You are more likely to succeed by being entirely cooperative towards the mediator, whether or not you agree with his approach. Promote interest-based negotiation and creative settlement options, engage in brainstorming, separate people issues from problem issues, and look for objective and independent or external criteria to justify settlement proposals; understand how to reciprocate; find ways to cross the last gap, justify splitting differences, and advance the last offer.

Dealing with Opposing Lawyers

- Keep your eyes on the ultimate objective of the process. It is to achieve a settlement.

- Clearly say what you really mean.

- Learn what your opponent really means.

- Do not assume either party (including your own) does not have ulterior motives for taking part in the mediation, the most obvious being to discover information.
- Do not assume any inequality of power can be rectified because the mediator is present.

- Do not assume the other side will accept either information given or a proposal when made.

- Do not assume everything said at the mediation will in fact remain confidential – a party might use it indirectly, and parties may breach or waive confidentiality.

Once you have reached a settlement do not indicate in any way that you feel you have gotten the better of your opponent: convey only that it was a good deal for both parties. Never suggest that you might have made more concessions or accepted a lower offer.

Dealing With Your Own Feelings

You will undoubtedly have to deal with situations that make you feel uncomfortable on a personal level. This is perfectly normal, particularly when you have started from a bullish position in the advice previously given to your client about the strength of his case. Strategies that help include:

- Finding ways to save face when you retreat from a previously held position or advice.

- Establishing the reason for a change in your negotiating position: you need to justify it to yourself as well as the client and the mediator.

- Taking 'time out' to reflect.

5.23 Control of the Client

You should anticipate that getting to settlement may require the mediator to drive a wedge between you and your client, at least to the extent of undermining the advice you are giving, which the mediator may feel is acting as a brake on the momentum. He may try to take over emotional control of the client who may become confused, nervous, bewildered, or angry. Your job is to prevent hurtful or unwise decisions or actions by the client, and to protect him from the harmful actions of the other side. The mediator will be aware of this and may use one of a number of techniques to try and neutralise you as an advocate if he feels that you are being over protective or defending either an overly legal interest or a position that he believes the client needs to release. As an extreme this may include asking you to meet in private session with your opponent thus giving the mediator access to your client in your absence.

This problem arises because to an extent you will feel the client needs to be protected from the mediator as well as the other side, particularly if you take a bullish view of the merits of his case. Your attitude is likely to stem from an inability to see outside the 'Box' (see Fig. 1[20]). Look at his wider interests, and try to judge objectively whether the mediator is right – is the client better off with you taking more of a back seat role or is the mediator going for broke because that is his personal agenda? You may find yourself in personal conflict since you will feel that you are there to perform your job and should be seen to be doing what you are paid for. However there may come a point at which you have to let go.

Equally you may consider that the other side or the mediator is being reasonable and your client recalcitrant and irrational, and you are unable to make him see what is by any standards a good deal for him and one unlikely to be achieved as the outcome of litigation. It is then that you must use the mediator as a foil to prevent the likely conflict between your views and your instructions.

Neither of these scenarios are uncommon, and the novice mediation advocate should not worry unduly should they occur. The mediator will be aware of these dynamics. There is no reason why you should not be alert to them also.

Consider that part of the process, indeed part of the ritual, is that mediation will help the parties learn more about themselves and each other. The best way to settlement is if both parties have a change of heart – the mediator will be aiming for compromise plus reconciliation. Otherwise if parties maintain an 'all or nothing' approach they will head irrevocably towards trial.

5.24 The Settlement Agreement

It is essential that the parties secure a concluded agreement that is workable, comprehensive, (both as to the dispute and any wider issues which have been introduced,) and enforceable. As your client's advocate it is vital that you get the form of the agreement right. As his lawyer it is part of your role to ensure that the settlement is enforceable. The terms must be certain, specific, effective, practical and complete, in particular dealing with who is to do what, when, and with what precise consequences. A provision will usually need to be inserted detailing what to do if one side or the other fails to adhere to the agreement or if it proves to be unworkable.

---

[20] See p.16.

It is as well to take a draft containing the likely heads of agreement with you and, if litigation is running, a general form of stay order. If the compromise contains terms found in a recognised standard form or precedent do not forget to bring it with you. Otherwise you will be forced to locate it, probably at a highly inconvenient time for doing so.

As you near settlement you should begin to draft the proposed agreement in your caucus room. Discuss the structure, form and contents with your client as early as possible, since you can formulate the structure as the mediation progresses. This will help focus on the details and will place the client's personal agenda in context.[21] At this point – prior to the actual agreement – your client must be clear about the practicalities of its implementation.

Be careful to strike a balance between too little, and too much detail. Do not be overly pedantic. Remember it is likely to be either quite late or very late, at the end of a long day. You may wish to keep the mediator informed of progress in drafting the agreement, and certainly where any problems arise.

While the document is being settled you should ask the decision maker in your party precisely who should be the signatory. Do not assume that you are signing it yourself, or do so without seeking express authority, irrespective of the fact that you are likely to have sufficient implied authority as a matter of law.

You may wish to consider the introduction of certain standard clauses irrespective of the nature of the settlement. These should deal with:

- confidentiality;

- any relevant choice of law or jurisdiction;

- the entire agreement between the parties;

- a default mechanism to deal with future disputes;

- whether, if there is a breach of this agreement, the original cause of action should be reinstated.

The settlement-specific clauses need to be certain as to:

---

[21] See York, Stephen D, *Preparing Your Client for Mediation* CEDR Resolutions issue 17 Summer 1997.

- payment: who pays, to whom is payment made, and how much;

- the form in which payment is to be made;

- whether payment is to be immediate or in stages;

- the mechanism for default of payment;

- the provision of interest;

- the costs of the litigation;

- the costs of the mediation;

- any public statements;

- the discontinuance or withdrawal of proceedings;

- any special clauses dealing with enforceability;

- who is the signatory, his status or authority.

There will be occasions when the parties can do no more than agree outline heads of agreement, but this should be avoided wherever possible. Saving an hour at the end of the mediation by agreeing outline heads of agreement exposes the parties to the risk of further disputes in which the argument shifts from its original subject matter to contesting what has been agreed. It is essential that the intention of the parties is made plain, and there is at least sufficient detail to ensure that an impartial reader would have a clear idea of precisely what has been agreed. If there is no time to put in the complexity of the mechanics of the transaction, or, for example, the tax implications have not been advised upon or worked out, at least draw a distinction between the agreement itself and the mechanics for performing it.

5.25 Time-Limited Mediations

In a sense all mediations are governed by limits on time. However many litigants and their advocates may first be introduced to mediation by being asked to participate in court-annexed schemes in circumstances where the parties have not agreed to mediate beforehand.

It is possible for parties to agree that a mediation should be limited in time to three or four hours, or a half-day without using a court-annexed scheme. This may be intended as a cost-saving device because there is only a single or narrow issue to be negotiated, or the parties mistakenly assume that if agreement cannot be reached in that time, it is unlikely to be reached at all.

In either case how is the advocate to deal with the curtailment or concentration of a process, which seemingly requires the time to pass through certain phases, including time for detailed negotiations? The answer depends to an extent on the approach of the mediator. Some will try to run the mediation in precisely the same way as if there were no time constraints. If he does he will try to compress the same events and process into shorter lengths of time, hoping to arrive at a satisfactory result. However more experienced and more confident mediators will probably jettison less important parts of the procedure and concentrate on the more important ones. For example he may either get rid of or limit the opening plenary session. In addition it may be that a guillotine is put on private caucusing. Certainly the preliminary posturing by both sides will be reduced, and offers expected far sooner than in a full day mediation. In other words the mediator will adopt a more focused approach to the management of the process and will discourage exhaustive discussion of the issues.

As you might expect, time limited mediations have a higher failure rate, particularly where the court has bounced an otherwise unwilling participant into trying them. However, in the hands of an experienced mediator, who is capable of successful time management, this process offers the client real value for money, in that there are no venue costs and none relating to the administration of a mediation service provider. In addition both court-annexed schemes and practising time-limited mediators will charge fees that are fixed.

As in all mediations the key to success is in the amount of pre-mediation preparation that can be completed. The fact that time is limited does not mean that a representative can avoid doing the necessary preparation. Quite the contrary is true. Before you attend you should have a thorough knowledge of the strengths and weaknesses of your own case, including arguments on liability and quantum, interest and causation; you need to know much the same about the case of your opponent; you need detailed information on the costs position of both sides, both historic and projected. Thus you will want to know the costs to date, the likely time to trial, and the likely duration and costs of the trial.

There will be an extremely limited bundle of core documents made available to the mediator, often consisting of nothing more than the statements of case. If there is time in advance the mediator may contact you beforehand, but again, that is unlikely. Under court-annexed schemes he will be paid extremely low rates. Fixed price fees in the private sector also allow for very little pre-mediation reading in by the mediator.

Before arriving you should be well aware of what to bring and how you are going to proceed. Your tactics will be far less sophisticated. But in each phase of the mediation the other side has to be persuaded that there is something in it for them.

Make a list of objective criteria: establish what it is you want by 7 p.m. (or 2 p.m.) that you haven't got now. Then consider the process: how to get what you want in a way that is most effective. Take a view of the most efficient use of your time, and that of any other attendees. Put short time fragments into a framework. Know what high figure and what low figure to request when the mediator asks for your position. That will be your negotiation range. Be able to explain to the mediator why there is a gap between the figures. Know how much it will cost to fight the gap, particularly whether the gap is less than the cost of going to trial. That may be the determinative factor in accepting the last offer or walking away.

If you are acting for insurers ask them to provide their risk cost analysis. The mediator may well ask for this. He will certainly ask the defendants what sort of a settlement they are looking for, and hope to move it into the claimant's negotiating range.

Remember that short as it is, it is still the client's day in court. Help negotiate a settlement with which he can be comfortable at the end of the session. Do not allow him to be bullied into an agreement simply because of the shortage of time. Ensure that he understands and is happy, albeit reluctantly, with any offer by the other side, which you believe cannot be improved upon.

PART 6

Mediation Privilege and Confidentiality

Chapter 6

MEDIATION PRIVILEGE AND CONFIDENTIALITY[1]

6.1 The Existence of Mediation Privilege

Within the development of modern civil/commercial mediation one of the clearest views we have of the creeping juridification of mediation by courts is the examination of privilege and confidentiality attaching to the mediation process, and, in doing so, consideration of the future compellability of the mediator. In the UK, the USA and Pacific Rim countries mediation trainers and mediator service providers have long proceeded on the basis that the mediator is not compellable at trial as a witness of the contents of a previous mediation of the dispute, whether the outcome was a settlement or otherwise. This sense of security for mediators is borne out of the contractual protection usually given by the parties in the mediation agreement. For the industry, the very essence of mediation depends upon the participants in the process being confident they can be as frank at all times and open with each other and the mediator as they would wish without fear that anything they said, or any document they produced solely for the purposes of the mediation, or any concession they may choose to make in the course of exploring a settlement, might subsequently be admitted into evidence in later court proceedings.

The LMDC Practice Direction, the FCT Rules and AMDC Practice Direction, and the Kano and Kaduna Protocols all support the principle that court-annexed mediation in Nigeria is confidential and privileged.

The common law countries are divided in their approach to what protection the courts will give to mediation in this respect. According to the analysis of Michel Kallipetis QC, there are two distinct views: some jurisdictions consider that mediation is 'no more than assisted without prejudice negotiations' while others consider that mediation has an entirely separate privilege of its own. In the first, the courts have regarded mediation privilege

---

[1] For this chapter I am greatly indebted to Michel Kallipetis QC FCIArb, a leading mediator and past Chairman of the Bar ADR Committee, for permission to draw upon a note on this subject provided to the Hong Kong Bar Association in November, 2009.

or confidentiality as subject to all the usual challenges with which we are familiar, and which, for convenience are listed below. In the second, some jurisdictions regard mediation privilege as absolute and will not admit any evidence at all of what transpired in a mediation, while others, though recognising the existence of such a privilege, permit the courts to admit evidence 'in the interests of justice'.

The law in Nigeria on this question has yet to be established with any degree of certainty.

Given the increasingly widespread use of mediation, and the greater judicial encouragement to mediate rather then litigate, the whole question of mediation confidentiality and privilege needs seriously to be reviewed and some form of consensus achieved.

In England and Wales the courts have now intervened to consider this aspect of mediation on a number of recent occasions. A slightly wider starting point may usefully be found in the analysis of the law on 'without prejudice' negotiations contained in *Unilever plc v Proctor and Gamble*,[2] on the court's approach to the admission of statements made in without prejudice negotiations in subsequent litigation. There, the plaintiff wished to use statements made in a without prejudice meeting to support an action to restrain a threatened infringement of a patent on the basis of alleged threats made in that meeting. Laddie J's decision to strike out the proceedings as an abuse was upheld by the Court of Appeal. Walker LJ reviewed all the modern authorities and summarised the major principles [page 2444 D to 2445 G] as follows:

> (1) When the issue is whether without prejudice communications have resulted in a concluded compromise agreement, those communications are admissible: *Tomlin v Standard Telephones and Cables Ltd*[3]

> (2) Evidence of negotiations is also admissible to show that an agreement apparently concluded between the parties during the negotiations should be set aside on the ground of misrepresentation, fraud or undue influence: *Underwood v Cox*[4]

> (3) Even if there is no concluded compromise, a clear statement made by one party to negotiations on which the other party is intended to

[2] [2000] 1 WLR 2436.
[3] [1969] 1 W.L.R. 1378.
[4] (1912) 4 D.L.R. 66.

act and does in fact act may be admissible as giving rise to an estoppel: See Neuberger J in *Hodgkinson & Corby Ltd v Wards Mobility Services Ltd*[5]

(4) Apart from any concluded contract or estoppel, one party may be allowed to give evidence of what the other said or wrote in without prejudice negotiations if the exclusion of the evidence would act as a cloak for perjury, blackmail or other 'unambiguous impropriety'. However, the court would only allow the exception to be applied in the clearest cases of abuse of a privileged situation. *Forster v Friedland*[6]

(5) Evidence of negotiations may be given (for instance on an application to strike out proceedings for want of prosecution) in order to explain delay or apparent acquiescence, albeit that the exception is limited to the fact that such letters had been written and the dates at which they were written. *Walker v Wilsher*[7]

(6) The exception for an offer made expressly "without prejudice save as to costs" is clearly recognised as an express or implied agreement between the parties to vary the public policy rule: *Rush & Tompkins v GLC.*[8]

Kallipetis believes the observations of Robert Walker LJ (at page 2448H to 2449B), where that judge reiterated that the without prejudice rule is founded partly in public policy and partly in the agreement of the parties, are of particular importance to the question of mediation privilege. The modern approach is to protect admissions against interest made in without prejudice negotiations, but

> "to dissect out identifiable admissions and withhold protection from the rest of without prejudice communications (except for a special reason) would not only create huge practical difficulties but would be contrary to the underlying objective of giving protection to the parties "to speak freely about all the issues in litigation both factual and legal when seeking a compromise and, for the purpose of establishing a compromise, admitting certain facts"
>
> (quoting Lord Griffiths in *Rush v Tomkins*[9])

---

[5] [1997] F.S.R. 178.
[6] C.A. (Civil Division) Transcript No. 205 of 1993.
[7] 23 Q.B.D. 335.
[8] [1989] AC 1280.
[9] [1989] A.C. 1280 at 1300.

As has been said earlier in this work, *Halsey v. Milton Keynes General NHS Trust*[10] was a seminal decision of the England and Wales Court of Appeal giving encouragement to parties to use mediation to resolve their disputes. While principally concerned with the costs sanction on parties who refuse unreasonably to mediate, Dyson LJ made wider observations on the use of mediation at [14]:

> "We make it clear that it was common ground at the outset (and we accept) that parties are entitled in an ADR to adopt whatever position they wish, and if as a result the dispute is not settled, that is not a matter for the court. As is submitted by the Law Society, if the integrity and confidentiality of the mediation process is to be respected, the court should not know, and therefore should not investigate, why the process did not result in agreement."

Subsequently, in *Reed Executive plc v. Reed Business Information Ltd,*[11] that court was asked to look at without prejudice correspondence to establish a claim for costs alleging one party had unreasonably refused to mediate. The Court of Appeal rejected any suggestion that *Halsey* had changed the substantive law, namely that protection given to without prejudice negotiations will not be removed by the court save in exceptional circumstances.[12]

In *Venture Investment Placement Ltd v. Hall*[13] the court granted an injunction to prevent disclosure of the contents of a without prejudice discussion. Judge Reid QC rightly observed [at paragraph 11]:

> "Mediation proceedings do have to be guarded with great care. The whole point of mediation proceedings is that parties can be frank and open with each other, and that what is revealed in the course of mediation proceedings is not to be used for or against either party in the litigation, if mediation proceedings fail".

6.2 Challenges to Mediation Privilege

However there have been some recent decisions where the courts have allowed a party to introduce in subsequent litigation evidence of what

---

[10] [2004]1 WLR 3002.
[11] [2004] 1 WLR 3026 per Jacob LJ @ [14].
[12] Law as set out in *Walker v Wilsher* (1889) 23 QBD 335 .
[13] [2005] EWHC 1227 (Ch)

transpired in a mediation. The trend has been to follow the 'without prejudice' line and admit the evidence either where the parties have themselves waived their privilege, or where the court has been persuaded that the evidence was admissible under one of the exceptions set out by Walker LJ in *Unilever plc v Proctor and Gamble.*

In *Brown v Patel*[14] a Mrs Rice purported to sell a property to Mrs Patel. Mrs Rice's trustee in bankruptcy, Mr Brown, brought proceedings under s.339 of the Insolvency Act against Mrs Patel alleging that the sale to her was at an undervalue. Mrs Patel denied this, and a three-day trial was set. A mediation took place shortly before trial, for which the parties signed a standard form ADR Group mediation agreement which provided (among other things) that:

(a) confidentiality would apply to statements and documents prepared for the mediation save those already disclosed in the litigation, and

(b) no settlement would be legally binding unless reduced to writing and signed by each party.

The mediation failed to give rise to a written settlement signed by each party. A preliminary issue at the trial was whether there has been an enforceable concluded settlement, and the judge decided to hear evidence about what happened at the later stages of the mediation, even though he recognised that he might later rule that such evidence was inadmissible. He turned first to the without prejudice rule and exceptions to its effect. He described mediation as "*assisted without prejudice negotiation*", with no special privileged status. Although it was argued that some kind of special mediation privilege exists or is beginning to emerge, he found no extant authority for this, even though he saw that the need for such a privilege might arise for consideration in the future. On the basis that he regarded mediation as a without prejudice negotiation, he held that the exceptions to the without prejudice rule which allowed evidence to be admitted, also apply to mediation.

Applying the decisions in *Muller v Linsley & Mortimer*[15] and *Tomlin v Standard Telephones and Cables,* the judge held that a court can find and enforce a binding contract reached by means of without prejudice negotiations and concluded that he was required to consider events, documents and offers, otherwise without prejudice, in order to make such a ruling.

---

[14] [2007] EWHC 625 (Ch).
[15] [1996] PNLR 74.

Among the many arguments which the judge rejected as reasons why he should not hear the evidence of what transpired in the mediation were the following:

> (a) Clause 1.4 of the mediation agreement expressly stated that no settlement was legally binding unless reduced to writing and signed by the parties. As this had not occurred, it followed that there had been no settlement, and it was thus otiose to receive evidence as to whether any agreement had been reached, as, unless it complied with the self-imposed formalities of the mediation process, no court could find there to be an (otherwise) enforceable contract of settlement.
>
> (b) The confidentiality provisions of the mediation agreement prevented the parties from giving evidence about what happened.

However, as the court had rejected the first argument, the second ground for seeking to exclude enquiry into what had transpired, was effectively undermined, and it was conceded that this provision could not prevent an enquiry into whether a concluded agreement had been reached within what the judge regarded as simply without prejudice negotiations.

The judge decided that although an offer had been 'left on the table' which had been accepted by the trustee, the offer was not certain enough in its terms; also, the provisions of clause 1.4 of the mediation agreement were not met. He therefore concluded that the parties had agreed terms 'subject to contract'. He rejected the argument that, by agreeing to leave an offer open for acceptance, Mrs Patel had varied or waived the terms of clause 1.4. Vitally, he accepted that offers were frequently left open at this stage, so that a valid offer and acceptance the next day would still be bound by the mediation agreement as a settlement reached in the mediation.

In the U.K. during 2007 and 2008 the trend seemed to be leaning against protecting the existence of mediation confidentiality. In *Cattley v Pollard*[6] a party to a mediation was ordered to give disclosure of mediation documents which were relevant to the issue of issues in subsequent proceedings. In *Earl of Malmesbury v Strutt and Parker*[7] the judge made a ruling on costs after considering, among other things, evidence led by both parties as to the offers each had made at a prior mediation.

However a different result occurred in *Cumbria Waste Management v Baines Wilson*.[18] There the Department for the Environment, Food and Rural Affairs

---

[16] [2007] Ch 353.
[17] [2008] EWHC 424 (QB).
[18] [2008] EWHC 786.

(DEFRA) were facing a series of claims arising out of the foot and mouth epidemic in the spring and summer of 2001 which caused a crisis in British agriculture and tourism. They settled an early claim by Cumbria at mediation. Dissatisfied with the amount of the DEFRA payment, Cumbria sued the solicitors who had drafted their original contract. Those solicitors sought disclosure of the mediation papers in order to explore the reasonableness of the settlement reached. Inevitably they relied on *Muller* to overcome DEFRA's assertion of without prejudice privilege. But the Judge was able to find that the truth or falsity of statements made in the mediation *would* be at issue in the claim against the solicitors. DEFRA successfully objected that statements made at the mediation could once revealed effectively be used as admissions in the upcoming claims by other similar companies. The solicitors could not bring themselves within the *Muller* exception to the without prejudice rule and disclosure was declined.

The widest debate in this area has been prompted by the decision of Mr Justice Ramsey in *Farm Assist Ltd v DEFRA (No.2).*[19]

In that case the judge refused to set aside on her application, a witness summons issued against leading mediator, Jane Andrewartha, to give evidence of the circumstances in which a settlement had come about in a mediation in which she was engaged, where the liquidator of Farm Assist was challenging its enforceability some four years after the event on the ground of the settlement at the mediation having been procured by DEFRA through economic duress.

DEFRA reacted to the allegation by seeking disclosure of all documents in Farm Assist' s possession which contained the legal and expert advice it had received leading to the decision to settle with DEFRA at the mediation; this to include advice given during and after the mediation, whether or not the mediator was present. Farm Assist objected on the ground that legal professional privilege protected it from disclosure. DEFRA argued that Farm Assist had waived such privilege by bringing proceedings against them which made material Farm Assist's thinking at the mediation.

In *Farm Assist Ltd v DEFRA (No.1)*[20] Ramsey J. had previously held that such advice was not disclosable by virtue of legal professional privilege and the issue of proceedings did not of itself amount to an implied waiver by the liquidators of Farm Assist. The Judge also declined to strike out the claim, and accordingly the focus of the parties' attention turned to whether the

---

[19] [2009] EWHC1102 TCC
[20] [2008] EWHC 3079 TCC; [2008] All ER (D)124

mediator could herself be called as a material witness to any alleged pressure brought to bear by DEFRA on Farm Assist by way of economic duress. She would have been present at any joint meetings in which relevant remarks may have been made; she would have carried offers and information between the parties, and discussed terms of settlement privately with them.

Since there had been no reported case in the UK of a mediator actually having been compelled to give evidence, whether a witness summons should stand is an important question, particularly here where both parties consented to the mediator being called (the liquidators agreed as the mediator had already indicated that she had neither notes nor any independent recollection of the contents of the mediation).

The relevant signed mediation agreement (of 2003) expressly provided for confidentiality as to the existence of the mediation and in relation to all information arising in relation to it including any settlement terms, documents covered by specific "without prejudice" privilege, and that the mediator should not to be called "*as a witness, consultant, arbitrator or expert in any litigation or arbitration in relation to the Dispute, and the Mediator will not act voluntarily in any such capacity without the written agreement of all the parties*".

The judge found as a matter of interpretation that the restriction on calling the mediator as witness as drafted was confined to 'the Dispute' – and not wide enough to cover a different dispute, namely whether economic duress had been deployed by one of the parties to procure settlement during the mediation. *Practitioners are accordingly advised to check with care the wording in more recent drafts of standard form mediation agreements for the ambit of restrictions imposed on party use of the mediator after the event.*

On broad considerations of the existence of confidentiality and privilege in mediations the judge concluded by reference to existing authorities as follows:

(1) *Confidentiality:* The proceedings are confidential both as between the parties and as between the parties and the mediator. As a result even if the parties agree that matters can be referred to outside the mediation, the mediator can enforce the confidentiality provision. The court will generally uphold that confidentiality but where it is necessary in the interests of justice for evidence to be given of confidential matters, the Courts will order or permit that evidence to be given or produced.

(2) *Without Prejudice Privilege:* The proceedings are covered. This is a privilege which exists between the parties, who can waive it. It is not a privilege of the mediator.

(3) *Other Privileges*: If another privilege attached to documents which are produced by a party and shown to a mediator, that party retains that privilege and it is not waived by disclosure to the mediator or by waiver of the without prejudice privilege.

Applying the present situation to his findings the judge found the parties had agreed to waive "without prejudice" privilege and that the mediator had disclosed her limited documentation; that an allegation of wrongdoing at the mediation was at the core of the claim; the clause in the relevant mediation agreement purporting to prevent the mediator from being called was not effective to prevent her from being called on this issue; the mediator has said that she had no helpful recollection of what happened at the mediation; the mediator had an enforceable right to confidentiality unless she should be called as a witness "in the interests of justice".

Having decided the central allegation of economic duress inevitably involved consideration of what the mediator said and did, and that her absence of recollection did not of itself justify not calling her for this to be tested out, he found "*as an exception*" *to* the mediator's right to confidentiality that "*the interests of justice lie strongly in favour of evidence being given of what was said and done*".

While practitioners will appreciate the importance of the mediator having been found to have an independent right to enforce confidentiality, the decision is questionable, if not wrong. Given that on any occasion where a party is dissatisfied with the outcome of a mediation - either where there are grounds to impeach a settlement he or she no longer wishes to be bound by, or the conduct of the opposing party is complained of, or there is merely an argument on liability for costs – he or she would wish to compel the mediator to provide evidence in support, it is difficult to see on what basis the judge found this situation an exception to the general rule he himself has established.

The judge sought comfort for the existence of an exception to the mediator's right of confidentiality from the judgment of Sir Thomas Bingham MR in *Re D (Minors) (Conciliation: Disclosure of Information)*[21]. However, as Michel Kallipetis QC comments in the *Mediator Magazine*,[22]

> "While acknowledging that in *Re D* the court was clearly dealing with a different position, Ramsey J does appear to have ignored the three

---

[21] [1993] Fam 231.
[22] *Mediators Awake: the Ongoing Debate over Mediation Privilege* Michel Kallipetis QC *Mediator Magazine* July 2009.

express reservations which the Master of the Rolls made, namely: 1. The decision was solely concerned with the welfare of children; 2. The decision was only concerned with privilege "properly so called...and has nothing to do with duties of confidence and does not seek to define the circumstances in which a duty of confidence may be superseded by other public interest considerations;" 3. The Court of Appeal "deliberately stated the law in terms appropriate to cover this case and no other. We have not thought it desirable to attempt any more general statement. If and when cases arise not covered by this ruling, they will have to be decided in the light of their own special circumstances".

Ramsey J also referred at length to the decision of HH Judge Frances Kirkham (also another trained mediator) in *Cumbria Waste Management v. Baines Wilson* [2008] EWHC 786, which the mediation community hailed as a welcome recognition that mediation privilege was to be upheld by the Courts. Curiously he did not refer to her unequivocal decision that the mediator should not be required to give evidence of what transpired in a mediation."

Thus at the time of writing the debate on mediation privilege remains confused and open. This decision has attracted wide interest.[23] Commentators generally agree that it is also likely to be incompatible with the European Directive on Mediation. However it will not be clarified in the Court of Appeal, at least not in the Farm Assist case, since the parties had come to terms even prior to Ramsey J handing down his decision, which makes the value of the authority itself questionable.

The England and Wales Civil Mediation Council issued a Guidance Note for mediators (Mediation Confidentiality - 8th July 2009) which suggests that mediation agreements should continue to specify that the mediation proceedings are conducted on a "without prejudice" basis; should continue to make it clear that what is said during mediation proceedings will be confidential; and should not restrict the circumstances in which a mediator cannot be compelled to give evidence in court *(sic)*.

---

[23] *Calling all Mediators: a review of Farm Assist v DEFRA* Tony Allen, *CEDR Resolutions Magazine* July, 2009 (www.cedr.com); *Farm Assist: Mediators Get Another Dose of Disclosure* Bill Woods QC *Mediator Magazine* July 2009; *Mediation Privilege?* The Hon. Mr Justice Briggs, *New Law Journal*, 3rd and 10th April 2009.

PART 7

Costs Issues

Chapter 7

COSTS ISSUES

A number of costs issues arise in the context of mediation, which are considered under the following topics:

- Mediation Costs
- Litigation Costs and ADR
- Adverse costs awards for a party's failure to mediate

7.1 Mediation Costs

Mediation does not operate in a vacuum. As a process it is entirely contractual, either in the private sector or under the supervision of one of the Multi-Door Courthouse schemes and hopefully, it succeeds in producing a further enforceable contract which settles the dispute between the parties. That being so it is for the parties to contract between themselves who will be responsible for the costs of the mediation. These include the costs of the mediator or neutral, any separate charge by an MDC service provider for administration or for room hire and refreshments, and the costs of party representatives and experts or other professional participants, for example accountants. If the mediation is organised into sessions, for example as in Abuja, there may be a separate fee per session.

Most standard form mediation agreements provide for the costs of the mediation to be met by the parties equally, and usually provide for payment of at least part of the fee in advance. MDCs charge what is in effect an entry fee for the service. There is nothing to prevent parties negotiating something different, between themselves and this occasionally happens where there is substantial inequality of arms, or a party is trying to induce the other side to come to mediation at all. During the course of the mediation a party may make it a term of the settlement that the agreement be varied to the extent that the mediation costs are provided for.

The costs of the mediation should properly be defined in the mediation agreement to avoid confusion. It may be the case that parties will return their own contribution to the cost of the mediator/neutral and the room hire, but if the dispute proceeds to litigation afterwards, they may try to recover their legal costs of the mediation as costs in the litigation.

7.2 Litigation Costs and ADR

When deciding whether to mediate, the issue of costs, particularly what costs a client is likely to recover, is usually a crucial consideration. Before considering this issue, it is important to remember that mediation is not cheap *per se*: it is an attractive alternative to litigation, which either proceeds to trial or at least has a substantial amount of costs expended upon it in the stages leading up to trial.

However the assertion by the mediation industry that mediation presents substantial cost savings by comparison with full-scale litigation is based on the assumption that the mediation will succeed. Should the mediation fail, or merely create a momentum towards settlement but which requires further steps to be taken in the litigation, the costs of the mediation will have to be aggregated with the litigation costs. If that occurs the costs of a failed mediation may be significant.

There are a number of reasons why mediations can be costly. These might include the following:

- Over the last few years the mediation process has been getting far more sophisticated in the hands of the lawyer representatives. Thus representatives approach (and should approach) the preparation for a mediation in the same way as a preparation for a trial, albeit with different procedures and using different advocacy techniques; they must allot adequate preparation time, including a pre-mediation conference with the client as necessary to identify the true negotiating parameters.

- Fees must take into account pre-appointment preparation, to include settling a case summary for the mediator and possibly a reply to that of the other side, and either voluntarily or where directed by MDC Rules, having personal communications with the mediator in advance of the appointment.

- In assessing hearing fees the litigator should be conscious of the fact that even mediations starting early in the morning may not conclude until well into the evening. It may be necessary to have a fee for the day with an additional hourly rate for after-court hours, alternatively a fee for a day and a half, or a separate fee for each session if that model is used.

- In addition it will have to be decided whether expert evidence will be necessary for the mediation, and if so the form it should take, and the directions if any, for pre-appointment exchange of reports or summaries. This may extend to property, tax or other accountancy advice on the nature and operation of the proposed settlement

- Witness statements or at least summaries may be necessary.

- As with arbitration, the parties are directly contributing to the costs of the mediator and the venue.

- There may be ancillary costs (hidden or open) which are payable to the mediation service provider (e.g. cost of catering, photocopying etc). An MSP is likely to build in a profit element into its administration fee; the MDC will just have a set charge.

On the other hand, mediations can and generally should be cheaper than litigation, and the flexibility of the mediation process is a reason why costs savings can be achieved. For example:

- The speed of the process restricts the amount of chargeable time likely to be incurred.

- The absence of formal structure means that the parties are free to choose the procedure, including the degree of formality or otherwise. They will certainly wish to dispense with matters that can result in a significant cost saving.

- There is no formality about third party claims or other additional parties. The procedure is thus far less expensive than a multi-party claim in litigation.

- The mediation is not a trial or tribunal: since the process is non-adjudicatory no findings need be made. Evidence, disclosure and documentation are substantially reduced and may be dispensed with altogether.

- There are no costs associated with the delivery of a judgment or consideration of an appeal.

- Moreover, the litigation may be suspended by agreement or by order during the mediation process to prevent further litigation costs accruing outside the mediation.

7.3 The Recoverability of Costs

Any analysis of what costs might be recoverable has to take into account all the situations in which a client might have incurred costs, including the costs of the mediation and of the litigation.

Costs of the Mediation in the Litigation

Parties have the freedom to choose how costs flow in mediation. The conventional principle in litigation that the loser pays the winner's costs, subject to the discretion of the Court – see, for example, Ord 49 r.6 of the Lagos Rules - is often alien to a resolution process whose fundamental approach is that both parties feel that they have achieved a benefit from participation. As has been suggested above, ordinarily each party will pay an equal share of the costs of the mediation to the service provider/MDC in advance, unless agreed otherwise, and a clause acknowledging liability for a share of the mediation costs will be contained in the mediation agreement. This avoids the cost of the mediation becoming an issue within the mediation. Parties can make it an issue if they wish but this will be an extra and unnecessary sticking point, which may impede settlement. Thus, unless otherwise agreed, parties to a mediation should expect to pay in advance for half the costs of the mediator, the room hire and any service fee to the mediation service provider, and pay their own costs of legal representation.

Litigation Costs in the Mediation

Liability for past litigation costs forms part of the claim being mediated. It is an issue that parties' representatives *must* confront before the mediation. Thus parties to a mediation are not properly prepared unless they attend knowing:

- The amount of costs they have incurred to date (including the costs of the mediation) - this needs to be as specific as possible.

- A good estimate of the likely costs that will be incurred to the end of the trial if necessary.

- A reasonable estimate of the recoverable/irrecoverable element of their total costs on detailed assessment or taxation by the Court, if sought (on the standard and indemnity bases of assessment).

In addition, either before, or during, the mediation each party ought to obtain from any other party details of that other party's costs, including an estimate of their costs to date, of their likely future costs, and of the recoverable/irrecoverable element of their total bill.

Mediation Costs in the Litigation

Should the mediation fail or the litigation not be settled until after the mediation process has concluded, the legal costs of the mediation will usually be claimed by the successful party as part of his litigation costs. This remains something of a grey area, particularly where the mediation is not court-directed. However two frequently deployed arguments, with which representatives should be familiar, are as follows:

- The mediation agreement is a complete collateral contract which stands outside the litigation and accordingly self-regulates the costs. To the extent that the mediation agreement does not specify the parties' liability for costs, they are borne by the party incurring them. If this argument succeeds, then the costs provided for within the agreement e.g. that each party pay a specified proportion of the costs of the mediator, the room hire and any service fee to the mediation service provider would be provided for but that all other costs would be irrecoverable.

- The mediation has narrowed down the issues in dispute which should be reflected in appropriate costs' order having regard to the court's discretion under Ord.49 r. 6 Lagos Rules and Order 53 r. 3 FCT Rules.

- Ordinarily the court cannot open up what occurred within the mediation for the purpose of exercising its discretion as to costs in the litigation. As was discussed in Part 6, the starting point remains that the contents of the mediation process are wholly without prejudice. However, a number of UK costs decisions (e.g. *Shirayama Shokusan v Danovo*[1] and *Halsey v Milton Keynes General NHS Trust*[2]) suggest that the court is entitled to make an assumption of what may have occurred had a mediation taken place when it did not do so.

7.4 The Relevance of Court-Directed Mediation

Each of the principal Multi-Door Courthouses has put in place a protocol for either directing parties to ADR or requiring the respondent to a 'walk-in'

---

[1] [2003] EWHC 390 (Ch); [2004] 1 WLR 2985.
[2] *Op.cit* [2004] 1 WLR 3002.

application for ADR to justify why ADR, and mediation in particular, should not take place.

The courts have directed the parties to undertake mediation with apparent zeal, often as part of their case management powers under Ord. 25 r.2(c) Lagos Rules or Ord. 17(a) FCT Rules. By so doing, they arguably risk undermining the consensual process of mediation.

Perhaps recognising this danger in the UK, the courts there have in a number of cases since 2004 made clear that a party could not be ordered to submit to mediation as this would be contrary to Article 6 of the European Convention on Human Rights, most prominently *Halsey v Milton Keynes NHS Trust.* However a tension remains between two principles, namely the courts' desire to achieve higher levels of settlement by mediation and its recognition of a party's right to have "his day in court". The principal mechanism under which both principles are observed is by the use of adverse costs orders in appropriate circumstances for a party's failure to mediate. Representatives in every case have to be astute to ensure that their client's conduct does not expose it to adverse costs orders under the general discretion of the High Court.

7.5 Adverse Costs Awards for a Party's Failure to Mediate

The mechanism for forcing parties to evaluate their position on ADR/ mediation is the impact of the discretionary costs regime under the High Court Rules attaching to each of the venues throughout Nigeria at which an MDCH operates. This is reinforced by those imperatives under which High Court judges mandate parties at last to consider mediation as part of an ongoing drive throughout the country to provide enhanced, more timely and more cost-effective access to justice to both applicants and respondents, but particularly in FCT and Lagos, Kano, Abia, Kaduna and Delta States. Thus it is a mandatory requirement of the Civil Procedure Rules that judges have some regard to the conduct of the parties in deciding costs issues, and where there is an ADR centre should ordinarily enquire whether the parties attempted to use it.

In the UK following the decision of the Court of Appeal in *Dyson v Leeds City Council (No.1)*[3] in which reference was made to the overriding objective

---

[3] [2000] CP Rep 42.

to deal with cases justly, and to the court's duty to manage cases, including "taking a strong view about the rejection of encouraging noises we are making" by imposing adverse costs orders, the case law developed quickly in favour of ADR. A particular feature of the subsequent cases was that the courts took the opportunity of encouraging the disposal of cases by ADR in every field of law and indicated their readiness to reduce a successful party's costs if they had, without justification, rejected offers of mediation from their opponents. *Dyson* was followed by *R (Cowl and others) v Plymouth City Council* (see above).

Perhaps the high point of adverse costs orders in the Court of Appeal came with *Dunnett v Railtrack*[4] (Brooke, Robert Walker and Sedley LJJ). Here the claimant had rented a farm adjacent to the defendant's railway lines. An accommodation gate crossing the lines was left open and three of the claimant's horses were killed when they strayed onto the track. The claimant sought damages for negligence. The claim failed both at first instance and in the Court of Appeal. When granting permission to appeal, Schiemann LJ had strongly recommended the possibility of ADR, and in particular a mediated settlement. The claimant sought ADR but the defendant, which argued that it was confident of success and that it would derive no benefit from mediation, rejected this. Despite succeeding in the Court of Appeal, the defendant was deprived of its appeal costs. The court held that often in cases a claimant might be satisfied with an apology and an explanation of what had occurred, something which could be explored using ADR. It was emphasised that it was a lawyer's duty to further the overriding objective under CPR Part 1.1; if parties rejected ADR out of hand they would suffer the consequences when costs came to be decided.

In giving the leading judgment, Brooke LJ appears to have been influenced by policy considerations, as indicated by the following passage:

> "It is to be hoped that any publicity given to this part of the judgment of the court will draw the attention of lawyers to their duties to further the overriding objective in the way that is set out in CPR Pt 1 and to the possibility that, if they turn down out of hand the chance of alternative dispute resolution when suggested by the court, as happened on this occasion, they may have to face uncomfortable costs consequence."

It is also perhaps significant that there is no suggestion in the judgment that the claimant would have necessarily been satisfied with an apology or

---

[4] [2002] EWCA Civ 302 [2002] 1 WLR 2434.

explanation. Moreover the court expressly declined to look at such settlement offers as had been made notwithstanding the refusal to mediate.

The approach of the Court of Appeal in *Dunnett* was then applied in a number of later cases, including:

- *Neal v Jones Motors*[5] where a successful party's recoverable costs were reduced by £5,000 for failure to follow the court's recommendation to mediate.

- *Royal Bank of Canada v Secretary of State for Defence*[6] where Lewison J had to decide whether a break notice had been served by the defendant in a landlord and tenant case. The defendant won on the merits. However the claimant had expressed, on a number of occasions its willingness to mediate the claim. Although the Lord Chancellor's Department had made a formal pledge committing government departments and agencies to settle cases through ADR, the court noted that the defendant had not abided by that pledge. The judge held that a willingness to mediate was something which was significant in deciding where costs were to lie. Accordingly he made no order as to costs, thus penalising the winning government department.

- *Virani v Manuel Revert Y CIA SA*[7] where the Court of Appeal was required to decide in what currency the claimant's damages ought to be awarded. On the application for permission to appeal, the defendant appellant had been offered the Court of Appeal's mediation service by the single Lord Justice. Notwithstanding such offer, the appellant declined to enter into any form of mediation. This refusal attracted the penalty of the successful respondent's costs being assessed on the indemnity, as opposed to the standard, basis of assessment.

However not all courts slavishly followed *Dunnett*: in *Hurst v Leeming*[8] Lightman J stated that where an unsuccessful litigant sought to argue that his opponent should be penalised in costs for refusing an offer to mediate, such rejection had to be considered on its own merits; any such refusal would only escape sanction by the court if it could be shown that mediation in the particular circumstances had no real prospects of success. Despite Lightman J's obvious enthusiasm for ADR, he concluded that mediation in the present case had no real prospect of success by reason of the character and attitude of the

[5] [2002] EWCA Civ 1730.
[6] [2003] EWHC 1841 (ChD).
[7] [2003] EWCA Civ. 1651; [2004] Lloyd's Rep 4.
[8] [2001] EWHC (Ch) 1051 [2003] 1 Lloyds Rep 379.

party offering mediation and he therefore refused to penalise the successful party in costs. Although the judge's approach is more nuanced, one drawback is that it requires the court to consider what would have happened had there been a mediation. Given that many judges have very limited training in the mediation process, there is a risk that this exercise will be speculative.

A little later in *Societe Internationale de Telecommunications Aeronuatiques SC ("SITA") v Watson Wyatt; Maxwell Batley (Part 20 Defs)*[9] Park J was required to consider a costs application by an unsuccessful litigant, based on the successful party's refusal of three offers of mediation during the proceedings. The judge did not (in terms) use as his starting point the question of whether mediation would have had a real prospect of success. In fact he expressly distinguished both *Dunnett* and *Hurst v Leeming*. He found against the unsuccessful litigant on the issue. In reaching his conclusion that the refusal of offers to mediate was reasonable, he took account of the length of time allowed in the offer of mediation for preparation of the mediation by the offeree party, the offeror's objective, namely that the other party should make a contribution in a settlement involving a third party (rather than to dispose of the dispute between offeror and offeree), and the robust terms in which the offer of mediation was made.

In *Valentine v Allen, Nash & Nash*[10] the Court of Appeal determined the issue of costs on an unsuccessful appeal brought by the claimant in proceedings to restrain an alleged trespass to land. The court concluded that the fact that the claimant's offer of mediation was refused by the respondents did not detract from the usual order that an unsuccessful appellant was to pay the respondent's costs in resisting the appeal since it was clear that the respondents had made real efforts to settle the dispute.

This is a clear contrast on the facts to *Dunnett* where, it will be remembered, the court declined to look at alternative attempts to settle.

Matters were then clarified by the Court of Appeal in *Halsey v Milton Keynes General NHS Trust.*[11] In the first case (*Halsey*), a claim by a Fatal Accidents Act claimant was dismissed and the judge awarded costs to the defendant despite the fact that it had refused the claimant's invitation to mediate. The claimant then appealed on costs. In the second case (*Steel v Joy & another*) the first defendant was unsuccessful in contribution proceedings against the second defendant. The second defendant was awarded its costs although it

---

[9] [2002] EWHC Ch 2401.
[10] [2003] EWCA Civ 1274.
[11] *Op cit.* [2004] EWCA Civ 576 [2004] 1 WLR 3002.

had refused the first defendant's invitation to mediate. The first defendant appealed on liability and costs. The Court of Appeal dismissed the appeals on costs by the claimant in *Halsey* and the first defendant in *Steel v Joy*. In reaching its decision the court articulated the following principles:

- To oblige truly unwilling parties to refer their disputes to mediation would be to impose an unacceptable obstruction on their right of access to the courts.

- In deciding whether to deprive a successful party of all or some of its costs for refusing to go to ADR it had to be borne in mind that the burden was on the unsuccessful party to show why the general rule should be departed from.

- Such a departure was not justified unless it could be shown that the successful litigant acted unreasonably having regard to all the circumstances of the case.

However the court considered the following as important but non-exhaustive factors to be taken into account:

- The nature of the dispute: some matters were intrinsically unsuitable for ADR.

- The merits of the case: a party's reasonable belief that he has a strong case would be relevant to reasonableness of his refusal of ADR, for otherwise the fear of costs sanctions might be used to extract unmerited settlements. If his declared belief was in fact spurious or not reasonably held, the court would be astute to this point. Where a case was evenly balanced, a party's belief that he would win ought to be given little or no weight when considering a refusal was reasonable save that his belief must not be unreasonable.

- Whether other settlement methods had been attempted but rejected.

- Where the costs of the mediation would be disproportionately high.

- Delay: this might be relevant if mediation was suggested late in the day and the effect of accepting it at that stage would be to delay the trial.

- Whether the mediation had a reasonable prospect of success: this was a relevant but not determinative factor. The burden would normally be on the unsuccessful party to show that there was a reasonable prospect of success (cf. *Hurst v Leeming*).

- Whether the court had encouraged mediation: the more that the court had encouraged mediation, the more likely it was that the unsuccessful party would discharge the burden of showing the successful party's refusal was unreasonable.

- Public bodies were not in any special position.

One point left unresolved by *Halsey* was whether the courts could in future receive in evidence any "without prejudice" documents or negotiations passing between the parties when considering the reasonableness of a party's refusal to mediate.

In *Reed Executive v Reed Business Information*[12] the Court of Appeal decided that judges could not. *Halsey* did not change the law that "without prejudice" material remained inadmissible (unless both parties agreed). However on the issue of costs, any material marked 'without prejudice *save as to costs*' could be looked at by the court. As Jacob LJ indicated, the inability of the court to look at "without prejudice" material means that in some instances, the court cannot decide whether a party's refusal to mediate was reasonable.

In the instant case, the Court of Appeal did not think that the refusal of Reed Business Information ("RBI"), the successful appellants, to mediate before the appeal hearing was unreasonable. Since RBI had lost at first instance, they would have been negotiating from a position of weakness; moreover the proposal was made at a late stage; in addition it was satisfied that RBI had a reasonable (and as it turned out justified) belief in their prospects of success. In those circumstances the court concluded that the possibility of ADR was not a relevant factor to take into account on the question of costs.[13]

In *Daniels v Commissioner of Police For The Metropolis*[14] the Court of Appeal relied upon the guidance found in *Halsey* when dismissing a claimant's costs appeal. At first instance, the claimant, a police officer, had lost her personal injury claim against the defendant and was ordered to pay its costs. As part of her appeal, she contended that the defendant's refusal to

---

[12] [2004] EWCA Civ 887 [2004] 1 WLR 3026.
[13] Cf. *Burchell v Bullard* [2005] EWCA Civ 358; [2005] BLR 330. Where the Court of Appeal stated that a party should not ignore a reasonable request to negotiate before proceedings started.
[14] [2005] EWCA Civ 1312.

negotiate, as evinced by its rejection of her Part 36 offers to settle, was unreasonable and that accordingly it should be deprived of part of its costs. In dismissing the appeal, the Court of Appeal adopted the approach set out in *Halsey*. Recognising that not all of the principles identified in the earlier decision would be relevant where (as here) the issue was unreasonableness in refusing to negotiate, Dyson LJ found two that were germane, namely the merits of the case and whether the mediation would have had a reasonable prospect of success. He observed that it might be entirely reasonable for a public body to take the view that it would contest (what it considered to be) unfounded claims to deter others. He continued: "If defendants, who routinely face what they consider to be unfounded claims, wish to take a stand and contest them rather than make payments (even nuisance value payments) to buy them off, then the court should be slow to characterise such conduct as unreasonable so as to deprive defendants of their costs, if they are ultimately successful."

In *Hickman v Blake Lapthorn*[15] Jack J was required to consider Halsey in the context of a costs argument between unsuccessful defendants to a lawyers' negligence claim. The judge had already found the first and second defendants, the solicitor and barrister respectively, liable for negligence in the conduct of personal injury litigation. The solicitor contended that he had been prepared to mediate the claim before substantial costs were incurred but nothing had come of it because the barrister had refused to enter into negotiations or mediate. In those circumstances it was argued, the claimant's costs from that date should be paid by the barrister defendant only and not by both defendants. In rejecting that submission, the judge accepted that there was a strong possibility that a settlement could be achieved close to the sum eventually awarded. However, the solicitor defendant had not satisfied him that the barrister's refusal to mediate was unreasonable, particular having regard to the large difference between the defendants in valuing the claim. Refusing to take a "commercial" view of litigation was not, Jack J observed, necessarily unreasonable.

The situation in Nigeria is nascent, particularly outside the experience of the FCT and Lagos. However the judges have embraced ADR by taking upon themselves the power of compulsion, signalled in *Jabita* v. *Onikoyi*[16] where the High Court of Lagos struck out both the main claim and counterclaim and directed the parties to ADR stating:

---

[15] [2006] EWHC 12 (QB).
[16] [2004] All F.W.L.R. 1625.

I consider this an appropriate circumstance to call upon the parties to consider amicable settlement and / or alternative avenues of resolving their dispute… Once a dispute is aired in any High Court…as here, it loses its "innocency" and acquires a potential "baggage of judicial commentaries, orders and / or directions" …In this regard therefore, in striking out both main suit and counter claim and to facilitate alternative dispute resolution either at the Lagos Multi-door ADR Center or any other respected forum such as the Lagos Island Local Government Chieftaincy Committee or better still in-house amicable resolution…I direct…accordingly.[17]

If the courts are therefore content to strike out claims for want of addressing ADR then *a fortiori* they will consider issues of costs for failure to adopt ADR.

---

[17] Op.cit. @1653-1654

PART 8

Making a Market in Mediation Advocacy

Chapter 8

MAKING A MARKET IN MEDIATION ADVOCACY

Even after twenty years the civil/commercial mediation industry in the UK feels like part of a nascent market. In Nigeria mediation came into the dispute resolution market place only after 2002. It is virtually virgin territory for those who want to develop professional services and marketable expertise in this area, and therefore the history of the mediators in the UK market ought to provide a cautionary tale.

8.1 The Mediators

There are approximately 50 mediation specialists in Nigeria, firms and chambers, most of whom will be appointed as neutrals on MDC panels. There are well over 5,000 trained mediators within the jurisdictions of England, Wales and Scotland but probably no more than 80 would describe themselves as full time mediators, and many will travel for appointments internationally. A greater number, probably 200-300 will undertake as mediators regular, if sporadic, mediations as an adjunct to their other professional practices, whether as lawyers, property or construction professionals, or as expert witnesses. Beyond that there are substantial numbers who have completed training, observer or assistantships, and qualified, but who seldom are retained as mediators. Most mediators have practices that combine several different conflict resolution skills, i.e. mediation, facilitation, training, and writing or speaking to encourage mediation awareness, or at least unbundling mediation services by separating out the individual skills and applying them in wider areas.

At the time of writing, the UK the market is so oversupplied that if the number of commercial cases available were distributed evenly among accredited mediators, no mediator would be handling more than two or three a year. Under such market conditions, pricing is emotive, and competition sharp.

However, whether there is a glut of mediators in the market is supposed but, in fact, only arguable. The issue is not one of saturation, since the market is undoubtedly growing, but more one of uneven distribution of work and market segmentation. Like most nascent markets, and almost all specialist markets, the perceived top practitioners get richer and have more visibility than others in the field.

The mediation industry has created a pyramidhic structure. At the very tip are the stars of mediation. Those highly successful, highly sought-after, relatively highly paid professionals are at the pinnacle of their careers for a reason. These were either the innovators who created a new business model for mediators during the early 1990s, or else the professional mediators who were among the second wave, training in the mid 1990s, who then carved out a practice by reason of price, expertise in a particular subject matter of work, quality of service or even force of personality. Work gravitates towards them by virtue of their experience and their reputation, and this notwithstanding the immense amount of choice now available in the market, particularly choice based on price. The concept of mass personalisation works for mediators just as well as it works for supermarket shampoo – every user can choose who they want in an open, unregulated market.

Most newer mediators lack the dedication, skills, mindset *and preparation* to build a practice. They attempt to gain experience by volunteering or getting involved with community mediation. However working without pay is not generally effective as a way of generating business. Logic offends the idea that mediation clients will someday decide to pay for services they previously received for free. What is likely to be more effective is offering the market sampling, that is offering a portion of your expertise for free in exchange for building a relationship and trust.

In reality the whole of the mediation industry undersells itself. *Mediation is a vital service that adds enormous value to the lives and businesses of people and deserves decent remuneration.* Practitioners should be able to create both a profitable practice, make a good living and serve others.

8.2 What Should Mediators and Advocates Charge?

Writing in *The Mediator* magazine in September, 2008 in which he presented the first published breakdown of senior mediators' charge out rates, Matthew Rushton argued that on an objective basis, given the relative workload of mediators and lead representatives or advocates on the day of the mediation, mediators should not be charging clients any less than party representatives. Doing so is justifiable not just on workload, but also on any value-added analysis. On a major commercial dispute, therefore, where litigators are billing anywhere from say UK £2,750 - £6,500 (say N630,000 – N1.5m over the course of a ten-hour day), mediators should bill the same, and that achieving parity with the highest paid lawyers in the room is a minimum obligation to the profession. Whether this sum should be billed to each party or split between them raises more complex questions. On a value-added basis, economists and accountants contacted by *The Mediator* believed mediators would be justified in doing so. Likewise, as a proportion of the legal spend in a case, the mediator's fee is often so small that doubling it would make little difference.

In AMDC the Neutral is billed out according to his experience at anything from N25,000 to N250,000 per mediation session.

Although the market rate undervalues the service mediators bring, devising a strategy to resist bargaining on price is a real challenge in a market where there is a strong perception of surplus practitioners. Over the course of a day's mediation the bracket of mediators who might expect to work on the same cases charge an average of 60% of partner rates. Hour for hour, the financial value the UK's best mediators attach to themselves is equivalent to a mid-level City of London associate. And where parties split the cost, in the case of a two-party dispute the mediator's cost to the client is half that of a mid-level associate, and frequently less in multi-party disputes. Even before approaching the question of what value mediators can bring to disputes, given these facts, the conclusion that mediators have priced their services at too low a rate is hard to avoid.

Although it may be said that mediators are only charging what the market will sustain, pricing in the mediator marketplace follows a number of patterns characteristic of a nascent market in which prices have yet to find their correct level. Where relevant benchmarks and precedents don't exist, pricing always involves an element of guesswork because both buyer and seller lack the information necessary to judge the value of the service correctly.

For the new entrant trying to develop practice as a specialist mediation advocate similar considerations may apply.

Nascent markets, of course, mature and evolve as the market grows more familiar with a new product. A number of factors unique to the mediation marketplace could be frustrating this process of price correction. First, intelligence on pricing is hard to come by. To form a clear view of the market, mediators need a wide frame of reference, and although mediators might discuss pricing on a one-to-one basis, groups and panels have been justifiably wary of such discussions for fear of exposing themselves to allegations of price-fixing and anti-competitive conduct. Secondly, mediation, for all its infinite flexibility and variety is sold – especially at the lower end of the market – as a fixed-price commodity irrespective of the qualities of the mediator. Defining rates relative to the sums in dispute creates more pricing clusters and resists the market's attempts to define a meritocracy.

Insufficient data serves to keep prices at an inefficient level which does the market little credit, and puts too much work into the hands of too few. Mediators generally, and paradoxically service providers, would benefit from better market intelligence.

8.3 What Mediators do Charge

Mediators generally quote day rates which fall into broadly similar bands when adjusted for the fact that some mediators quote on the basis of a 10-hour day and others assume an eight-hour day. Charging for additional time on the day is relatively common, although some mediators take the view that their fee is for the duration of the mediation regardless of how late it runs.

How mediators choose to bill for preparation time varies widely. The accepted wisdom is that clients are more comfortable with a fixed fee, and some mediators offer a package which incorporates preparation time into their day rate. Some incorporate all necessary preparation into their day rate; others allow a certain amount of preparation and travel, varying from three to ten hours.

The obvious downside to package deals such as these is that if more preparation is required the mediator will either have to bill by the hour, defeating the object of a packaged rate, or lose out financially. In the latter instance the mediator has a financial disincentive to prepare adequately. The reality, however, is that most mediated disputes can be prepared for adequately in three to five hours or less.

In order not to price themselves out of the market, one common practice among mediators is to quote a lower day rate for disputes where the sums involved are relatively small, and a higher rate for a higher subject matter.

Rushton contends that with a few exceptions, the market demonstrates just how insecure the profession is. He suggests that the underlying sentiment behind offering reduced rates, not charging for hours over the quoted-for eight or 10-hour thresholds, and not billing for too much preparation time is that mediators should be grateful for the work at any price.

Though it is right and proper that the mediators differentiate themselves from the legal profession, the contrast with regard to representatives' fees is especially stark. The leading law firms do not compete on cost; they focus instead on getting better quality work from fewer clients, aggressively sidelining low-paying clients. They are also more bullish about charging for their time because they are confident of their quality of service and value they deliver. Equally, law firms have been unapologetic in raising their fees steeply over the last decade.

The legal market is open and highly competitive, and good information is available about the qualities and competencies of both firms and individual lawyers. The result is that the top law firms do not drop their rates to that of high street solicitors to act for owner-managed businesses. Rushton believes that the only way in which the market can mature and enable prices to harden is to identify with certainty who the top mediators are (which is not difficult) and have those mediators limit themselves to the top cases and charge properly for them (which is plainly likely to be more of a challenge). Without this the market will remain weak.

8.4 Mediation Advocacy

If the history of the civil/commercial mediator market in the UK has any lesson for representatives, it is not to sell mediation advocacy as a new market, but as a new specialist skill within the existing dispute resolution market. This would avoid the difficulties in market share and the uneven distributions of work associated with the nascent market, and hopefully, prevent a pyramidhic structure developing. Of more importance is to identify a clear distinction between the services offered by the mediator and the role of the mediation advocate.

The essence of this book has been to persuade readers that the mediation process is a highly sophisticated form of managed negotiation in which greater, rather than less preparation will be needed to play an active role as lead negotiator, advocate and strategist for your client, by comparison with trial presentation. That being so the mediation advocate will be using his or her usual litigation or consultancy charge-out rate as a base figure for charging. Specialist rates may, and generally should, attract a premium.

Following the pattern of mediator charges is certainly not recommended. Advocates, and particularly counsel, may roll together the cost of a pre-mediation conference and preparation into a single base fee, but professional charging should be in line with the value they bring to the task.

8.5 Where will your Practice come from?

Many practitioners who wish to undertake more mediation or ADR activity follow the same trend as mediators. They engage in *'Field of Dreams'* marketing, hoping that work will turn up: they associate themselves with panels and training providers. They offer pro bono work in the community sector. They wait for referrals from other lawyers: many lawyers like to refer ADR work to others because that is the dispute resolution world they know best. Even if you are a litigator it is going to take a long time to build a full-time practice that way.

Waiting for your national, regional, and local mediator or professional practice associations to educate the public and create work for you is not an attractive option. Most practitioner associations do not have enough resources to make this a reality in the near future and it is debatable whether that should even be their job.

So stop waiting for someone else. Start creating your own reality, in just the way you expect your mediation clients to take responsibility for their own lives, behaviours, and decisions. Market the process and your expertise positively, and start right now. Among regular clients and among your firm or chambers. Talk up the concept, and base your ADR practice on your own strengths and the kinds of tasks you enjoy. Build on what you already know and value in order to do the work you want.

Appendix 1

MEDIATION AGREEMENTS

Example 1.
Model agreement of RICS Dispute Resolution Services reproduced by kind
permission of the Royal Institution of Chartered Surveyors

RICS

[STANDARD FORM MODEL]
MEDIATION AGREEMENT
VERSION /

This Agreement is made the   day of   201

Parties:

Party A

....

Party B

....

[Party C etc

....

(Together referred to as **"the Parties"**)

The Mediator/s

....

(A term which includes any Assistant or Pupil Mediator)

[And]

[RICS Dispute Resolution Services of Surveyor Court, Westwood Way, Coventry,
CV4 8JE]

In relation to a mediation to be held

On ....

At ....

("The Mediation")

Concerning a dispute between the Parties in respect of[1]

....
....
....
....

("The Dispute")

IT IS AGREED by those signing this Agreement that:

1   The Parties will (unless and until one of the Parties withdraws from the Mediation, or it is otherwise determined) attempt in good faith to resolve the Dispute by mediation and will take all such steps as may be necessary to participate fully in the mediation process, including the taking of all preparatory steps for the mediation appointment. The provisions of the DRS Code of Procedure set out in Appendix 1 as supplemented by the Terms & Conditions shall apply to the Mediation and are incorporated in and form part of this Agreement.

2   The Parties warrant that the signatory to this Agreement has the authority to bind the respective Party and all others present at the mediation appointment on that Party's behalf to bind that Party to observe the terms of this Agreement, and the Terms & Conditions, and also have authority to bind that Party to the terms of any settlement agreement.

3   The Mediator may in his or her absolute discretion give such directions for the conduct of the Mediation as he or she thinks fit. Such directions shall be communicated in writing to the Parties' Representatives for the time being as soon as reasonably practicable.

4   The mediation appointment shall take place as set out above. If the Dispute has not been resolved at the end of the time allotted then, with the agreement of all the Parties and the Mediator, the appointment may be continued or may be resumed at such time and place as the Parties, the Mediator [and DRS] may agree.

---

[1] Provide sufficient detail to identify the complaint/s of the Party seeking a remedy

5   The procedure at the Hearing shall be determined by the Mediator in consultation with the Representatives. In the event of any disagreement the decision of the Mediator shall be final.

5.1 Unless otherwise agreed by the Parties the language in which the Mediation shall be conducted shall be English and this Agreement and any settlement agreement shall be governed by the law of England and Wales and the Parties agree to submit to the exclusive jurisdiction of the Courts of England and Wales as regards any claim or matter arising under or in relation thereto. the Heads of Agreement.

5.2 In the event that no settlement is reached by the Parties all the Parties' rights shall be reserved and shall remain in all respects unaffected by the Mediation save to the extent provided in this Agreement.

6.   The Parties, their Representatives, their advisers and the Mediator and Assistant Mediator (if any) shall keep confidential and shall not reveal save as required by law and insofar as may be necessary to bring into effect or enforce the settlement agreement:-

6.1.1 any written summaries of the Parties' cases;
6.1.2 any statements whether oral or written made in the course of the Hearing;
6.1.3 any concessions or admissions of law or fact;
6.1.4 that any settlement has been reached;

6.2 The Mediation shall be confidential and shall be treated as though the same was a negotiation conducted upon a "without prejudice" basis with a view to settling proceedings and shall be privileged according to law.

6.2.1 No recording or other verbatim record shall be made or kept of the Mediation.

6.3 All documents, written case summaries, written submissions, written concessions or admissions of law or fact or written statements (whether prepared specifically for the purposes of the Mediation or not) used or disclosed for the purposes of the Mediation and in the possession of the Mediator shall be destroyed after the conclusion of termination of the Mediation.

7.   The Parties shall not be permitted to rely upon any expression of opinion, advice or comment made by the Mediator in the course of the Mediation in or for the purposes of any legal or similar proceedings or any form of alternative dispute resolution in relation to the Dispute or any matter related to or concerning the subject matter of the Mediation.

7.1 The Parties will not call the Mediator or any employee or consultant of DRS as a witness nor require them to produce in evidence any records or notes relating to the Mediation in any litigation, arbitration or any other formal process arising from or in connection with the Dispute and the Mediation, nor will the Mediator nor any DRS employee or consultant act or agree to act as a witness, expert, arbitrator or consultant in any such process.

8.   The Parties shall be responsible for the Mediator's fees [and the fees of DRS] in accordance with the Terms & Conditions.

8.1   Unless otherwise agreed in writing all the costs of the Mediation, the fees and expenses of the Mediator (which expression shall include the Assistant Mediator where one is appointed), the costs of the appointment [and the administrative charges and costs of DRS] including all Value Added Tax shall be borne by the Parties in equal shares. However each Party further agrees that any court or tribunal may treat any such fees and costs and each Party's legal costs as costs in the case in relation to any litigation or arbitration where that court or tribunal has power to assess or make orders as to costs, whether or not the Mediation results in the settlement of the Dispute.

8.2   In the event that the Parties settle the Dispute before the mediation appointment or for any other reason the appointment does not take place or is adjourned, but after fees payable in advance have become due (whether paid or not) DRS and or the Mediator shall be entitled to retain or receive payment (as the case may be) of any irrecoverable expenses incurred   together with   the following additional charges:-

(1)   Cancellation 5 working   days or more before the date fixed for the commencement of the Hearing – No additional charges.
(2)   Cancellation 3-4 working days before the date fixed for the commencement of the Hearing - 25% of the daily rate plus the fees for any preparation time actually spent by the Mediator.
(3)   Cancellation less than 3 working days before the date fixed for the commencement of the Hearing - 50% of the daily rate plus the fees for any preparation time actually spent by the Mediator.
(4)   The Parties shall responsible for all such fees, expenses and additional charges in equal shares   and DRS shall not be concerned or affected by any dispute or disagreement between the Parties or any of them as to who is responsible for the cancellation or adjournment of the Hearing.
(5)   For the avoidance of doubt DRS will act as the agent of the Parties in respect of any booking of accommodation, equipment hire or the like which the Parties may require for the purposes of the Mediation and the Parties shall be liable to indemnify DRS in respect of any such booking fees, equipment hire or the like which are incurred by DRS on their behalf.

Exclusions of Liability

9.   Neither DRS nor any of its employees, servants or agents nor the Mediator nor any Assistant Mediator shall be liable to the Parties in contract, tort (including negligence and breach of statutory duty) or otherwise howsoever except in the case of fraudulent misrepresentation or dishonesty for (i) any increased costs or expenses (ii) for any economic loss, loss of profit, business, contracts, revenues or anticipated savings or (iii) for any other loss or damage (including but not limited to special, indirect or consequential loss or damage)of whatever nature in respect of any act or omission in connection with the services provided by them.

9.1 No responsibility is assumed by DRS nor by any of its members, servants or agents nor by the Mediator nor by any Assistant Mediator for the accuracy or completeness of any advice or opinion proffered (whether intentionally or not) in the course of the Mediation or for any assistance given in or about the content or drafting of any settlement agreement and the Parties acknowledge that they are not entitled to rely upon any such advice, opinion or assistance and must seek their own legal or other professional advice.

9.2 The Mediator and the Assistant Mediator where appointed act as independent service providers in the performance of their functions in connection with the Mediation and are not the servants or agents of DRS nor its representative(s) and the Parties hereby expressly acknowledge that the Mediator and the Assistant Mediator where appointed so act.

Signed:................................
On behalf of Party A

Signed:................................
On behalf of Party B

[Signed ....
On behalf of Party C etc]

Signed:................................
Mediator

[Signed:................................
On behalf of DRS]

APPENDIX

CDRS Code of Procedure

The Mediator's Position

1. The ultimate right to determine the procedure at the Hearing rests with the Mediator. He or she may in his or her absolute discretion terminate any meeting or discussion, limit the time for which any Representative may address him or her or otherwise act in any way seen fit with a view to the efficient, fair and orderly conduct of the appointment.

2. Neither the Mediator nor any Assistant Mediator will act as counsel, consultant, advisor or expert for any Party to the Dispute in relation to the Dispute nor in any other capacity in relation to the Dispute which might reasonably be considered to involve the use of confidential information to which he or she has become privy by reason of his involvement in the Dispute as Mediator or Assistant Mediator unless all the Parties agree in writing that he or she may so act.

Termination of the Mediation

3. Any Party to the Mediation may withdraw from the Mediation at any time and shall forthwith notify the Mediator, DRS as appropriate and the other Parties in writing. In the event of a Party withdrawing from the Mediation:-

   3.1. that Party shall remain liable for its share of the fees and charges in respect of the Mediation up to and including the date upon which written notice is received by DRS including such fees and charges payable in advance which have become due (whether paid or not) and DRS shall be entitled to retain or receive payment (as the case may be) of its administrative charges and any irrecoverable expenses incurred including any fees of the Mediator in respect of reading time or preparation;
   3.2. the remaining Parties to the Mediation (if more than one) may by notice in writing to the Mediator and or DRS agree to continue the Mediation as between themselves and if they do so agree shall in the same notice inform the Mediator and or DRS the issues remaining the subject of the Mediation.

4. The Mediator may in his or her absolute discretion determine for any reason that the Mediation ought to be terminated or adjourned and the Mediator shall not be required to give his or her reasons for so determining.

Parties' Own Costs

5. The Mediator has no power to award costs to or against any Party.

Example 2.

Model agreement of Littleton Chambers Dispute Resolution Services reproduced by kind permission of the Littleton Disputes Dispute Resolution Services Ltd.

MEDIATION AGREEMENT

No:

This Agreement is made the   day of   2010

1   The Parties will (unless and until one of the Parties withdraws from the Mediation, or it is otherwise determined) use their best endeavours to resolve the Dispute by mediation and will take all such steps as may be necessary to participate fully in the mediation process ("the Mediation"), including the taking of all preparatory steps for the mediation hearing ("the Hearing"). The provisions of the LDRS Code of Procedure set out in Appendix 1 hereto as supplemented or varied by this Agreement shall apply to the Mediation and are incorporated in and form part of this Agreement.

2   The Parties appoint as Mediator the person named in the Mediation Particulars.

3   "Representative" shall mean the person for the time being nominated on behalf of any Party as acting on its behalf at and for the purposes of the Hearing. The Representatives for the Parties at the Hearing will be as set out in the Mediation Particulars or such other representatives as the Parties may notify to LDRS and each other from time to time. No Representative shall be permitted to represent any Party at the Hearing unless notification has been given to LDRS and to the other parties at least 24 hours prior to the commencement of the Hearing unless the Mediator in his absolute discretion permits such Representative to appear or all the Parties agree to such Representative appearing. Nothing in this clause 3 shall prevent any Party speaking on his own behalf or any employee, officer or partner (as the case may be) speaking on behalf of a Party which is a company, unincorporated association or firm (as the case may be) with the consent of the Mediator.

3.1 No Party shall instruct any member of Littleton Chambers to act for them in the Mediation or to represent them at the Hearing unless all other Parties to the Mediation consent in writing.

4   The Parties' respective Representatives at the Hearing shall have full authority to settle the Dispute and each Party hereby warrants that its representative at the Hearing shall have full authority to settle the Dispute.

5   Not less than 14 days before the date fixed for the Hearing or within such shorter time as the Mediator may in his absolute discretion direct each of the Parties shall submit to the Mediator and exchange with each other a written summary of its case together with supporting documents.

6   The Mediator may in his absolute discretion give such further or other directions for the conduct of the Mediation as he thinks fit. Such directions shall be communicated in writing to the Parties' Representatives for the time being as soon as reasonably practicable.

7   The Hearing shall take place at the date, time and place set out in the Mediation Particulars. If the Dispute has not been resolved at the end of the time allotted for the Hearing then, with the agreement of all the Parties and the Mediator, the Hearing may be continued or may be resumed at such time and place as the Parties, the Mediator and LDRS may agree.

8   The procedure at the Hearing shall be determined by the Mediator in consultation with the Representatives. In the event of any disagreement the decision of the Mediator shall be final.

9   The Hearing shall continue during the time allotted and shall determine upon the happening of any of the following events:-

9.1 The Mediator in his absolute discretion determines that no useful purpose would be served by continuing the Hearing;

9.2 The Mediator in his absolute discretion determines for any reason that the Mediation ought to be terminated or adjourned and the Mediator shall not be required to give his reasons for so determining;

9.3 One of the Parties withdraws from the Mediation;

9.4 The Parties reach agreement.

10 If agreement is reached between the Parties the same shall not be legally enforceable unless incorporated into written Heads of Agreement signed by them or by their Representatives who shall be deemed to have full authority to enter into such Heads of Agreement on their behalf.

10.1 Any such Heads of Agreement shall be legally enforceable by the Parties and the Parties agree to give effect to the terms thereof.

10.2 Unless otherwise provided in the Heads of Agreement, the Heads of Agreement shall be governed by and construed in accordance with English law and the Parties agree to submit to the exclusive jurisdiction of the Courts of England and Wales as regards any claim or matter arising under or in relation to the Heads of Agreement.

10.3 In the event that no Heads of Agreement are entered into by the Parties all the Parties' rights shall be reserved and shall remain in all respects unaffected by the Mediation save to the extent provided in this Agreement.

11

11.1 The Parties, their Representatives, their advisers and the Mediator and Assistant Mediator (if any) shall keep confidential and shall not reveal save as required by law and insofar as may be necessary to bring into effect or enforce the Heads of Agreement:-

11.1.1 any written summaries of the Parties' cases;
11.1.2 any statements whether oral or written made in the course of the Hearing;
11.1.3 any concessions or admissions of law or fact;
11.1.4 that any settlement has been reached;
11.1.5 the Heads of Agreement;
11.1.6 the fact that the Mediation has taken place, is taking place or is going to take place

PROVIDED that the foregoing
(i) shall not prohibit the disclosure of the matters set out in paragraphs 11.1.4 and 11.1.6 hereof insofar as may be strictly necessary to keep informed any court, other tribunal or other party to any dispute for the proper management of any litigation concerning or related to the dispute or disputes the subject of the Mediation

(ii) shall not prevent the Parties issuing and publishing any announcement or statement the terms of which and the place and method of publication of which they have all agreed.

11.2 The Mediation shall be confidential and shall be treated as though the same was a negotiation conducted upon a "without prejudice" basis with a view to settling proceedings and shall be privileged accordingly.

11.3 All documents, written case summaries, written submissions, written concessions or admissions of law or fact or written statements (whether prepared specifically for the purposes of the Mediation or not) used or disclosed for the purposes of the Mediation shall not be the subject of disclosure, in any legal or similar proceedings whatever provided that documentary evidence which would otherwise be subject to disclosure, inspection or production in such proceedings shall not be protected against disclosure, inspection or production by reason of its use or disclosure in the course of the Mediation.

11.4 All oral submissions, oral statements or oral concessions or admissions of law or fact made in or for the purposes of the Mediation shall be inadmissible as evidence in any legal or similar proceedings whatever provided that if they would otherwise have been admissible in such proceedings they shall not be rendered inadmissible by reason of having been made also in the course of the Mediation.

11.5 The Parties shall not be permitted to see or to inspect or to make use of the Mediator's or any Assistant Mediator's notes or any document prepared by them for the purposes of or in the course of the Mediation for the purposes of any legal or similar proceedings or in any form of alternative dispute resolution in relation to the Dispute or any matter related to or concerning the subject matter of the Mediation save in relation to any proceedings brought solely for the purposes of the enforcement of the Heads of Agreement and only insofar as they relate to any matters relevant to such proceedings.

11.6 The Parties shall not be permitted to call the Mediator or the Assistant Mediator (if any) as a witness in any legal or similar proceedings or in any form of alternative dispute resolution in relation to the Dispute or any matter related to or concerning the subject matter of the Mediation save in relation to any proceedings brought solely for the purposes of the enforcement of the Heads of Agreement and only insofar as any evidence they may give relates to any matters relevant to such proceedings.

11.7 The Parties shall not be permitted to rely upon any expression of opinion, advice or comment made by the Mediator in the course of the Mediation in or for the purposes of any legal or similar proceedings or any form of alternative dispute resolution in relation to the Dispute or any matter related to or concerning the subject matter of the Mediation.

12

12.1 Unless otherwise agreed in writing all the costs of the Mediation, the fees and expenses of the Mediator (which expression shall include the Assistant Mediator where one is appointed), the costs of the Hearing and the administrative charges and costs of LDRS including all Value Added Tax shall be borne by the Parties in equal shares. The Mediator shall be remunerated in accordance with the standard rates of LDRS from time to time or in accordance with any special terms agreed between LDRS and the Parties.

12.2 All fees, costs and charges of the Mediation shall be paid to LDRS which shall be responsible for paying the Mediator and meeting the expenses of the Mediation out of payments received but not otherwise.

12.3 The costs and expenses of the Mediation as estimated by LDRS shall be payable by the Parties in advance on dates fixed by LDRS. LDRS shall be at liberty to require the payment of further estimated costs and expenses from time to time. If the Parties fail to make payment in accordance with LDRS's requirements from time to time LDRS shall be at liberty to suspend the Mediation until payment in full has been made and to cancel any Hearing without prejudice to any other claims, rights and remedies which it may have.

The Parties will be invoiced for any additional sums not paid in advance and such invoice shall be paid within 14 days of its date. Late payments will bear interest at 5% per annum over Coutts & Co plc Base Lending Rate compounded with daily rests.

12.4 In the event that the Parties settle the Dispute before the Hearing or for any other reason the Hearing does not take place or is adjourned, but after fees payable in advance have become due (whether paid or not) LDRS shall be entitled to retain or receive payment (as the case may be) of any irrecoverable expenses incurred together with the following additional charges:-

Cancellation 5 working days or more before the date fixed for the commencement of the Hearing – No additional charges.

Cancellation 3-4 working days before the date fixed for the commencement of the Hearing - 25% of the daily rate plus the fees for any preparation time actually spent by the Mediator.

Cancellation less than 3 working days before the date fixed for the commencement of the Hearing - 50% of the daily rate plus the fees for any preparation time actually spent by the Mediator.

The Parties shall responsible for all such fees, expenses and additional charges in equal shares and LDRS shall not be concerned or affected by any dispute or disagreement between the Parties or any of them as to who is responsible for the cancellation or adjournment of the Hearing.

For the avoidance of doubt LDRS will act as the agent of the Parties in respect of any booking of accommodation, equipment hire or the like which the Parties may require for the purposes of the Mediation and the Parties shall be liable to indemnify LDRS in respect of any such booking fees, equipment hire or the like which are incurred by LDRS on their behalf.]

Exclusions of Liability

13

13.1 Neither LDRS nor any of its officers servants or agents nor the Mediator nor any Assistant Mediator shall be liable to the Parties in contract, tort (including negligence and breach of statutory duty) or otherwise howsoever except in the case of fraudulent misrepresentation or dishonesty for (i) any increased costs or expenses (ii) for any economic loss, loss of profit, business, contracts, revenues or anticipated savings or (iii) for any other loss or damage (including but not limited to special, indirect or consequential loss or damage)of whatever nature in respect of any act or omission in connection with the services provided by them.

13.2 No responsibility is assumed by LDRS nor by any of its officers servants or agents nor by the Mediator nor by any Assistant Mediator for the accuracy or completeness of any advice or opinion proffered (whether intentionally or not) in the course of the Mediation or for any assistance given in or about the content or drafting of any settlement agreement and the Parties acknowledge that they are not entitled to rely upon any such advice, opinion or assistance and must seek their own legal or other professional advice.

13.3 The Mediator and the Assistant Mediator where appointed act as independent service providers in the performance of their functions in connection with the Mediation and are not the servants or agents of LDRS nor its representative(s) and the Parties hereby expressly acknowledge that the Mediator and the Assistant Mediator where appointed so act.

14. This Agreement shall be governed by and construed in accordance with English law and the Parties agree to submit to the exclusive jurisdiction of the Courts of England and Wales as regards any claim or matter arising under or in relation to this Agreement.

Dated the   day of   2010

Signed:...................................
On behalf of First Party

Signed:...................................
On behalf of Second Party

Signed: ....
Mediator

Signed:................................. Director
On behalf of Littleton Dispute Resolution Services Limited

APPENDIX

LDRS Code of Procedure

The Mediator's Position

1. The ultimate right to determine the procedure at the Hearing rests with the Mediator or, as the case may be, the Joint Mediators. The Mediator may in his absolute discretion terminate any meeting or discussion, limit the time for which any Representative may address him or otherwise act in any way he says fit with a view to the efficient, fair and orderly conduct of the Hearing.

2. The Parties may appoint whomsoever they think fit to act as their Representative at the Hearing provided that not more than one Representative shall appear for any Party at the Hearing except in substitution for a previously notified Representative in accordance with clause 3 of the Littleton Chambers Mediation Agreement.

3. No formal record of the Hearing will be kept by the Mediator or any Assistant Mediator.

4. Neither the Mediator nor any Assistant Mediator will act as counsel, consultant, advisor or expert for any Party to the Dispute in relation to the Dispute nor in any other capacity in relation to the Dispute which might reasonably be considered to involve the use of confidential information to which he has become privy by reason of his involvement in the Dispute as Mediator or Assistant Mediator unless all the Parties agree in writing that he may so act.

5. The Mediator may at his discretion, but only at the request of all the Parties to the Dispute who have participated in the Hearing, suggest terms upon which the Dispute should, in his opinion, be settled. Such expression of opinion shall not be binding upon the Parties and shall not be relied upon in or for the purposes of any legal or similar proceedings or in or for any form of alternative dispute resolution in relation to the Dispute or any matter related to or concerning the subject matter of the Mediation. The Parties acknowledge that they are not entitled to rely upon the completeness or accuracy of any such suggestion and must seek their own legal or other professional advice as to the terms upon which the Dispute should be settled.

Other Proceedings etc

6. Unless the Parties expressly agree in writing entering into the Mediation Agreement shall not prevent any party from commencing or continuing any litigation or arbitration in relation to the Dispute.

Termination of the Mediation

7. Any Party to the Mediation may withdraw from the Mediation at any time and shall forthwith notify the Mediator, LRDS and the other Parties in writing. In the event of a Party withdrawing from the Mediation:-

7.1. that Party shall remain liable for its share of the fees and charges in respect of the Mediation up to and including the date upon which written notice is received by LRDS including such fees and charges payable in advance which have become due (whether paid or not) and LRDS shall be entitled to retain or receive payment (as the case may be) of its administrative charges and any irrecoverable expenses incurred including any fees of the Mediator in respect of reading time or preparation;

7.2. the remaining Parties to the Mediation (if more than one) may by notice in writing to LRDS agree to continue the Mediation as between themselves and if they do so agree shall in the same notice inform LRDS of the issues remaining the subject of the Mediation.

8. The Mediator may in his absolute discretion determine for any reason that the Mediation ought to be terminated or adjourned and the Mediator shall not be required to give his reasons for so determining.

Parties' Own Costs

9. The Mediator has no power to award costs to or against any Party. Each Party shall therefore bear its own costs and expenses of participating in the Mediation and attending at the Hearing.

For the avoidance of doubt this is without prejudice to the parties' respective rights to recover their costs and expenses of participating in the Mediation as costs of the litigation.

Appendix 2

PRACTICE DIRECTION ON
MEDIATION PROCEDURE

THE LAGOS
**MULTI-DOOR
COURTHOUSE**
...an alternative dispute resolution centre

CONTENTS
Introduction

1.   Application of the Practice Direction

2.   Commencement of Actions

3.   Request for Mediation

4.   Submission to Mediation

5.   The Mediation Agreement

6.   Appointment of the Mediator

7.   The Mediator's Qualification

8.   Role of the Mediator

9.   Role of Counsel

10.   Role of the Parties

11.   Role of the Courts

12.   Date, Time and Place of Mediation

13.   Representation of Parties and
       Attendance at Meetings

14.   The Mediation Process

15.   Confidentiality

16.   Settlement Agreement

17.   Enforcement

18.   Termination

19.   Expenses, Fees and Costs

20.   Fees of the Mediator

21.   Privacy

22.   Suspension of Running of Limitation
       Period under the Statue of Limitation

23.   Waiver of Liability

24.   Interpretation and Application of Articles
       Definition Section

INTRODUCTION

The Negotiation and Conflict Management Group (NCMG), the initiators of the Multi-Door Courthouse concept in Nigeria in collaboration with the High Court of Lagos established The Lagos Multi-Door Courthouse (LMDC) in June, 2002. This was in a bid to establish a Private-Public sector partnership.

Since inception the NCMG has administered the LMDC under The NCMG Centre for Dispute Resolution Rules. However, following the promulgation of the Lagos Multi-Door Courthouse (LMDC) Law in May 2007, it has become necessary for the Lagos Multi-Door Courthouse (LMDC) to have its own Practice Direction for mediation procedure.

"Pursuant to the powers conferred upon me by section 30 of the Lagos Multi-Door Courthouse Law and other powers enabling me in that behalf, I hereby make this Practice Direction on Mediation Procedure for the administration of mediation matters at the Lagos Multi-Door Courthouse. "

The Articles

ARTICLE 1   Application of the Rules

a) Whenever, by mutual agreement or contract, the parties have provided for or agreed to mediate existing or future disputes under the auspices of the Lagos Multi-Door Courthouse (LMDC), they shall be deemed to have made this Practice Direction a part of their agreement.

b) This Practice Direction shall apply to matters referred to the LMDC for mediation from High Court of Justice in Lagos State and other jurisdictions outside Lagos State, Federal Courts, Private persons, Corporations, Public Institutions and Dispute Resolution Organizations.

ARTICLE 2   Commencement of action (Mediation)

Walk- Ins
a) Any party or parties to a dispute may initiate mediation by filing with The LMDC a written request for mediation.

b) Upon receipt of such a request, the LMDC will contact the other party involved in the dispute and attempt to obtain a submission to mediation.

Court Referrals

c) Upon receipt of an Enrolment of Order from the referral court, the LMDC invites the parties to submit to the ADR Process.

Direct Intervention

d) The LMDC can also assist parties in the resolution of their disputes by extending an invitation to the disputing parties.

ARTICLE 3:   Request for Mediation

A request for mediation shall contain a brief statement of the nature of the dispute and the names, addresses, telephone numbers, telefax, email or other communication and references of all parties to a dispute and their representatives (if any) in the mediation. The initiating parties shall simultaneously file three copies of the request with the LMDC and one copy for every other party to the dispute.

ARTICLE 4   Submissions to Mediation

a) The other party on receipt of the Notice of Referral notifies the LMDC in writing within 7 days that it shall submit to the mediation in accordance with the Practice Direction on Mediation Procedure.

b) Upon the refusal to submit by the refusing party within the stipulated time to the ADR Process, the ADR Judge shall order the refusing party to appear before him/her and he/she shall make orders and give directives as shall be considered desirable in fulfilling the overriding objectives of the LMDC.

c) Where a party refuses to appear before the ADR Judge as stipulated in (b) above, this shall be treated as contempt of court and the ADR Judge shall give orders which include fines, cost in monetary terms etc or make other orders as may be considered appropriate under the circumstances.

ARTICLE 5:   The Mediation Agreement

The parties, the Mediator and the LMDC will enter into an agreement ("Mediation Agreement") in relation to the confidentiality and conduct of the mediation process.

ARTICLE 6: Appointment of the Mediator

a) Upon filing of a request for mediation, the LMDC will, subject to the parties' approval, appoint a qualified mediator from its Panel of Neutrals to serve or, alternatively, provide the parties with a short list of mediators from its Panel of Neutrals to choose from.

b) There shall be a single mediator appointed unless the parties or the LMDC advises otherwise.

c) If by mutual agreement of the parties, or the contract between them a mediator is named, or a method of appointing a mediator is stipulated, the mediator so named, or the method so stipulated shall be followed.

d) In the event that the parties are unable to agree within 7 days from the date of the notice initiating the mediation, as to who should serve as the mediator or on any issue concerning the conduct of the mediation, the LMDC will, at the request of either party, decide the issues for the parties having consulted with them.

e) The LMDC is authorized to appoint another mediator if both parties are not satisfied with the appointed mediator or if the appointed mediator is unable to serve or serve promptly.

f) The prospective mediator shall by accepting the appointment, be deemed to have undertaken to make available sufficient time to ensure the expeditious conduct of the mediation.

ARTICLE 7: The Mediator's Qualification

a) In appointing a mediator, such mediator must have considerable relevant experience in their particular field of Alternative Dispute Resolution practice and be trained and duly certified by a reputable and recognized organization such as NCMG, SPIDR, CEDR, AFMA etc.

b) No person shall serve as a mediator in any dispute in which that person has any financial or personal interest in the result of the mediation, except with the written consent of all parties.

c) Every prospective mediator shall, prior to accepting an appointment, disclose any circumstance likely to create a presumption of bias or prevent a prompt meeting with the parties.

d) The LMDC shall upon receipt of such information either replace the mediator or immediately communicate the information to the parties for their comments.

e) In recommending or appointing a mediator, the LMDC shall have regard to such considerations as are likely to secure the appointment of an independent, impartial and experienced mediator.

f) The mediator shall abide by the terms of the LMDC Practice Direction on Mediation Procedure, the Mediation Agreement and the Lagos Multi-Door Courthouse Code of Conduct for Mediators.

ARTICLE 8: Role of the Mediator

a) The role of Mediator is to assist the parties in an impartial manner in their attempt to reach an amicable settlement of their dispute. He/she does not have the authority to impose a settlement on the parties.

b) The Mediator should in his conduct of the mediation process take into account the circumstances of the case, the underlying interest of the parties and the need for a speedy settlement of the dispute.

c) The Mediator is authorized to end the Mediation whenever, in the judgment of the Mediator, further effort at mediation would not contribute to a resolution of the dispute between the parties.

d) The Mediator may assist the parties in drawing up a settlement Agreement.

ARTICLE 9: Role of Counsel

a) The role of counsel is to give regard and ensure clients' accord respect to notices, invitations and directives from the LMDC.

b) Ensure the appearance of his client at every Mediation session.

c) Explore with the client various options available so as to ensure speedy conclusion of the mediation process.

d) Respect the confidentiality of the Mediation session(s).

e) Embrace a cultural change and accept an advisory role while parties take the lead role in Mediation sessions

f)   Be cooperative and encourage his client to be cooperative during Mediation sessions to ensure a speedy resolution of the dispute.

ARTICLE 10:   Role of the Parties

a)   The role of Parties is to attend all mediation sessions either personally or by a duly authorized representative.

b)   Parties are expected to attend the ADR session in good faith without undue requests for adjournments or unwarranted delays.

c)   Parties must prepare adequately for an ADR session, be actively involved and be willing to explore various options towards settlement.

d)   Respect the confidentiality of the Mediation session(s).

e)   Cooperate fully with the mediator and the other party throughout the mediation process to ensure a speedy resolution of the dispute.

ARTICLE 11: Role of the Courts

It will be the responsibility of the Judges of the High Court of Lagos:

a)   To control and manage proceedings in Court and issue orders which would encourage the adoption of ADR methods in dispute resolution

b)   To mandatorily refer parties directly to the Lagos Multi-Door Courthouse (LMDC) to explore settlement of their dispute

c)   To ensure the adoption and enforcement of Terms of Settlement reached at the LMDC in the same manner as a Judgment or Order of Court.

ARTICLE 12: Date, Time and Place of Mediation

a)   The mediator shall in conjunction with the LMDC fix the date and time of each mediation session. The mediation shall be held at the appropriate office of the LMDC, or at any other convenient location agreeable to the mediator and the parties.

b)   The dates fixed by the mediator and the parties for each mediation session shall not exceed ten (10) days from the date of the last mediation session.

c) The mediator shall exercise all due diligence in encouraging the parties to reach a settlement within a maximum of three (3) mediation sessions.

ARTICLE 13: Representation of Parties and Attendance at Meetings.

a) Each party must be properly represented at every mediation session. Any party who is unable (for any reason whatsoever) to attend or make arrangements to be properly represented at a fixed mediation session must notify The LMDC at least 48 hours before the mediation session is scheduled to take place.

b) Failure to comply with this Article attracts a penalty fee of N10,000.00 (Ten thousand naira) per session missed or as may be directed by the ADR judge. The fee becomes immediately payable by the offending party.

c) Where a party fails to pay the penalty fees as stated above, this act of omission shall be treated as contempt of court and sanctions shall apply.

d) The parties may be represented by persons of their choice, provided such representatives have the authority which must be in writing to settle the dispute on behalf of the parties.

e) The names and addresses of such persons are to be communicated in writing to all the parties and to The LMDC before the first mediation session.

ARTICLE 14: The Mediation Process

a) The Mediator is authorized to conduct joint and separate meetings with the parties.

b) No formal record or transcript of the mediation shall be made without the prior consent of the parties

c) Each party shall cooperate in good faith with the mediator to advance the mediation possess as expeditiously as possible.

d) In addition, each party may send to the Mediator (through the LMDC) and/or bring to the mediation further documentation which it wishes to disclose in confidence to the Mediator but not to any other party, clearly stating in writing that such documentation is confidential to the Mediator and/or the LMDC.

e) At any stage of the mediation process, the Mediator may request a party to submit to him /her additional information as he/she deems appropriate.

f) If the parties are unable to reach a settlement at the mediation and if all the parties, or their representatives, so request and the Mediator agrees, the Mediator will produce for the parties a non-binding recommendation on terms of settlement. This will not attempt to anticipate what a court might order but merely set out what the Mediator suggests are appropriate settlement terms in all of the circumstances.

g) Efforts shall be made to conclude the mediation within 30 days of the appointment of the Mediator; which includes the signing of the Settlement Agreement by the parties and endorsement the Mediator and the ADR Judge/Referral Judge.

ARTICLE 15: Confidentiality

a) Every person involved in the mediation including, in particular the Mediator, the parties and their representatives and advisors, any independent experts and any other persons present during the meetings of the parties with the mediator, shall respect the confidentiality of the mediation and will keep confidential and not use (unless otherwise agreed by the parties and the Mediator) for any collateral or ulterior purpose:

   i) all information, (whether given orally, in writing or otherwise) produced for, or arising in relation to, or in connection with the mediation including the settlement agreement, except in so far as is necessary to implement and enforce any such settlement,

   ii) proposals made or views expressed by the Mediator,

b) All records, reports or other documents, arising in relation to the mediation will be without prejudice, privileged and not divulged or admissible as evidence or discoverable in any current or subsequent arbitration, litigation or other proceedings whatsoever except any document or other information which would in any event have been admissible or discoverable in such arbitration or litigation proceedings.

c) None of the parties to the mediation agreement will call the Mediator or the LMDC (or any employee, consultant or representative of the LMDC) as a witness, consultant, arbitrator or expert in any arbitration, litigation or any other proceedings whatsoever arising from, or in connection with or in relation to the dispute. The Mediator and the LMDC will not voluntarily act in any capacity without the written agreement of the parties.

d) All parties to the Mediation, including the Mediator, are bound by the Confidentiality Agreement even after conclusion of his/her service as Mediator or after conclusion of the Mediation.

ARTICLE 16: Settlement Agreement

a) When it appears to the Mediator that there exist elements of a settlement which would be acceptable to the parties, he/she may formulate terms of a possible settlement and submit to the parties for their observations. After receiving the observations of the parties, the Mediator may reformulate the terms of a possible settlement in the light of such observations.

b) Each party may, on his own initiative or at the invitation of the Mediator, submit to the Mediator suggestions for the settlement of the dispute.

c) If the parties reach an agreement upon a settlement of the dispute, they shall draw up and sign a written Settlement Agreement. Upon the request of the parties, the Mediator shall draw up or assist the parties in drawing up the Settlement Agreement.

e) The parties on signing the Settlement Agreement are bound by the terms of the agreement .

ARTICLE 17: Enforcement

Once reduced into writing and signed by the parties, the Settlement Agreement is forwarded for endorsement to the Referral Judge (court-referred matters) or the ADR Judge (Walk-in & Direct Intervention matters) and in accordance with Section 19 of the LMDC Law, 2007 and Order 39 Rule 4(3) of the High Court of Lagos State (Civil Procedure) Rules, it shall be deemed to be enforceable as a judgment of the High Court of Lagos State under Section 11 of the Sheriffs and Civil Process Law.

ARTICLE 18: Termination

The Mediation shall be terminated:

a) By the execution of a settlement agreement by the parties;

b) By a written declaration of the Mediator to the effect that further efforts at mediation are no longer worthwhile.

ARTICLE 19: Expenses, Fees and Costs

a) Parties are required to pay a non-refundable administrative fee upon submission of Statement of Issues or Statement in Response or as may be directed by the LMDC.

b) Parties are also required to pay Session Fees before the commencement of Mediation or as may be directed by the LMDC.

c) All other incidental expenses shall be borne equally by the parties, unless they agree otherwise.

d) The expenses of witnesses, if any, called by either side shall be paid by the party producing such witnesses.

e) Payment of these fees and expenses will be made to the LMDC in accordance with its fee schedule and terms and conditions of service.

ARTICLE 20: Fees of the Mediator

The amount and currency of the fees of the Mediator and the modalities and timing of their payment shall be fixed by the LMDC taking into consideration the amount in dispute, the complexity of the subject matter of the dispute and any other   relevant circumstances of the case.

ARTICLE 21: Privacy

a) Mediation sessions are private. Other persons may attend only with the permission of the parties and with the consent of the Mediator.

b) There shall be no stenographic or any other record of the Mediation process without the prior consent of the parties.

ARTICLE 22: <u>Suspension of Running of Limitation Period under the Statue of Limitation</u>

The parties agree that, to the extent permitted by the applicable law, the running of the limitation period under the statute of Limitation or an equivalent law shall be suspended in relation to the dispute that is the subject matter of the mediation from the date of the commencement of the mediation until the date of the termination of the mediation.

ARTICLE 23: <u>Waiver of Liability</u>

Neither the Mediator nor the LMDC shall be liable to the parties for any act or omission in connection with the services provided by them (Mediator/the LMDC), or in relation to the mediation, unless the act or omission is fraudulent or involves willful misconduct in which case only the individual person(s) directly responsible for the fraud or willful misconduct shall bear the consequent liability.

ARTICLE 24: <u>Interpretation & Application of Article</u>

a) Once the LMDC has the parties' agreement to submit a dispute to Alternative Dispute Resolution, it will administer the case under the LMDC Law, No 56, Vol. 40, 2007, its applicable rules of procedure or under such rules stipulated by the parties.

b) Beyond mediation, the LMDC might offer, (or the parties might choose) Arbitration, Executive Dialogue, Neutral Evaluation or any variation of these procedures on which the parties agree.

c) All articles herein shall be interpreted and applied by the LMDC.

<u>Definition Section</u>

In this rule, unless the context otherwise requires,

- "Alternative Dispute Resolution" (ADR) refers to a range of processes designed to aid parties in resolving their dispute outside the formal judicial proceedings.

- "ADR judge" refers to a serving Judge of the High Court of Lagos State who has been appointed by the Chief Judge of Lagos State to carry out such activities and functions as contained in these rules.

- "Mediation" is a process in which a third party neutral facilitates communications between parties to assist them in reaching a mutually acceptable resolution of their dispute; Mediator is the name given to the third party neutral.

- NCMG means the Negotiation and Conflict Management Group, the independent, non-profit and non governmental organization which founded the LMDC.

- An initiating party is the person who brought the matter to the LMDC.

- Panel of Neutrals refers to the list of Mediators, Arbitrators and Neutral Evaluators already screened and accredited by the LMDC provide Mediation and Arbitration services at the LMDC.

- AFMA means African Mediation Association. It is the organization set up by top African Dispute Resolution organizations to set standards for Mediation and Mediation Training in Africa.

- CEDR means the Centre for Effective Dispute Resolution. It is a UK based independent non-profit dispute resolution organization involved in Mediation Training and Conflict Management.

Dated this _____ day of _____2008

Hon. Justice A. Ade Alabi
Chief Judge of Lagos State.

Bibliography

Abel, Richard 'The Contradictions of Informal Justice' in *The Politics of Informal Justice* 1982 Academic Press, New York ed. Abel, R.

Abel, Richard L. Law Books and Books About Law (1973) 26 *Stanford Law Review* 175

Abramson, Harold I. *Mediation Representation* 2004 NITA

Bateson, David. Mediation and Adjudication in Hong Kong (1997) 63 *Arbitration* 243

Birch, Elizabeth *New Sophistications in Commercial Mediation,* ACI newsletter issue 9 Spring/Summer 2004

Birch, Elizabeth *The Historical Background to the EU Directive on Mediation* (2006) 72 Arbitration 1,57

Black D. and Baumgartner M.P. 'Toward a Theory of the Third Party' in *Empirical Theories about Courts* 1983 Longman New York ed. Boyum K. and Mather L.

Breitel, *The Quandary in Litigation* (1960) 25 MLR 225

Burgess, Heidi *Transformative Mediation* 1997 Conflict Research Consortium

Bush, Robert A. Baruch, and Folger, Joseph P. *The Promise of Mediation* Jossey-Bass, San Francisco 1994.

Burton, Frances. Dispute Resolution – an Integral *not* Alternative Process: the English and Canadian Experiences (2001) 1 *Journal of ADR, Mediation & Negotiation* 33.

Chartered Institute of Arbitrators' Mediation Compendium *From Small Acorns* 2nd Annual Mediation Symposium 29th October 2009 ed. Hudson-Tyreman, AD and Betancourt, JC

Cohen, Jerome A. Chinese Mediation on the Eve of Modernisation (1966) 54 *California Law Review* 1201

Commercial Court Committee Working Party on ADR 2nd Report, November 1998

Connerty, Anthony. The Role of ADR in the Resolution of International Disputes (1996) 12 *Arbitration International* 47

Coons, John. Approaches to Court-Imposed Compromise – The Uses of Doubt and Reason (1964) 58 *Northwestern Law Review* 750

Cunningham, Clark D. *The Lawyer as Translator, Representation as Text: Towards an Ethnography of Legal Discourse* 77 Cornell LR 1298

Damaska, Mirjan R. *The Faces of Justice and State Authority* YUP 1986

Dawson, John P. *A History of Lay Judges* Harvard University Press, Cambridge, Mass. 1960

Dingwall, Robert. Empowerment or Enforcement: Some Questions About Power and Control in Divorce Mediation in R. Dingwall and J.Eekelaar (eds) *Divorce Mediation and the Legal Process* OUP 1988

Dodson, Charles *Preparing for Mediation* (1997) 17 Resolutions, CEDR

Fisher, R, Ury W and Patton, B *Getting to Yes: Negotiating Agreement without Giving in* 2007 edn Random House Business Books

Folberg, Jay: *A Mediation Overview: History and Dimensions of Practice* (1983) 1 Mediation Quarterly 3

Folger J. and Bush R.B. 'Ideology, Orientation to Conflict, and Mediation Discourse' in *New Directions in Mediation* 1994 Sage Publications, Thousand Oaks, California eds. Folger J and Jones, T.

Folger J. and Bush R.B. *The Promise of Mediation: Responding to Conflict Through Empowerment and Recognition* 2nd edn 2006 Jossey-Bass, San Francisco.

Gaitskell, Robert. Current Trends in Dispute Resolution (2005) 71 *Arbitration* 288

Galanter, Marc *Justice in Many Rooms: Courts, Private Ordering and Indigenous Law* (1981) J.Legal Pluralism 1

Galanter, Marc 'The Radiating Effects of Courts' in *Empirical Theories about Courts* 1983 Longman New York ed. Boyum K. and Mather L.

Galanter, Marc *Reading the Landscape of Disputes: What We Know and Don't Know (And Think We Know) About Our Allegedly Contentious and Litigious Society* (1983) 31 UCLA L.R. 4

Galanter, Marc Adjudication, Litigation and Related Phenomena in *Law and the Social Sciences* 1986 Russell Sage Foundation ed. Lipson, L and Wheeler S.

Galanter, Marc *Compared to What?Assessing the Quality of Dispute Processing* (1989) 66 Denver L.R. vol 3 xi Reports of the University of Wisconsin Dispute Processing Research Program Workshop on *'Identifying and Measuring the Quality of Dispute Resolution Processes and Outcomes'*, Madison, July 13 and 14, 1987.

Galanter, Marc *A World Without Trials?* [2002] Journal of Dispute Resolution 1

Galanter, Marc *Planet of the APs: Reflections on the Scale of Law and its Users* (2006) 54 Buffalo L.R. 1055

Galanter, Marc *The Privatisation of Justice and the Vanishing Trial* paper, IALS WG Hart Legal Workshop 2006: The Retreat of the State: Challenges to Law and Lawyers

Golding, Martin P. Preliminaries to the Study of Procedural Justice in *Law, Reason and Justice* G. Hughes ed. New York NYUP 1969

Goode, Roy. 1997 Alexander Lecture. 'Dispute Resolution in the Twenty First Century' (1998) 64 *Arbitration* 9

Greatbach, David and Dingwall, Robert *Selective Facilitation: Some Preliminary Observations on a Strategy used by Divorce Mediators* (1989) 23 Law & Society Review 4.

Hall S. The Problem of Ideology in *Critical Dialogues in Cultural Studies* ed. Hall Routledge 1996

Hensler, Deborah *Suppose It's Not True: Challenging Mediation Ideology* (2002) J.Disp Resol. 81

Hicks, M.A. Restraint, Mediation and Private Justice: George, Duke of Clarence as 'Good Lord' [1983] *Journal of Legal History* 56.

Hill, Richard *Enforceability of a Mediation Clause* (1997) 63 Arbitration 302

Honeywell, Martin *Mediation and Theories of Change* CEDR Exchange, September 2005

Kaufman S., Elliott M. and Shmueli D. *Frames, Framing and Reframing* 2003 Beyond Intractability Knowledge Base Project

Kirkham, Frances. Judicial Support for Arbitration and ADR in the Courts in England and Wales (2006) 72 *Arbitration* 53

Lord Chancellor's Department   Report of the Advisory Committee on Legal Education and Conduct (ACLEC) 2003

Lim, L.Y. *Resolving Disputes by Mediation* Proceedings of the SBEM Silver Jubilee Arbitration and ADR Seminar, School of Building and Estate Management, National University of Singapore 21 January 1995.

Mackie, Karl *The Effective Mediator* CEDR seminar paper February 2002

Marinari, Marcello. ADR and the Role of Courts (2006) 72 *Arbitration* 49

Menkel-Meadow, Carrie *Is the Adversary System Really Dead? Dilemmas of Legal Ethics as legal Institutions and Roles Evolve* (2004) 57 CLP 85

Mnookin R and Kornhauser L *Bargaining in the Shadow of the Law: The Case of Divorce* (1979) 88 Yale Law Journal 950

Monberg, Tina *Handbook of Human Conflict Technology* 2007 Paragon Publishing

Murray, John S., Rau, Alan Scott and Sherman, Edward F. *Processes of Dispute Resolution: The Role of Lawyers* 1989 Foundation Press, Westbury, New York.

Nesic, Miryana *Mediation advocacy: how to keep it on track for results* Paper delivered at CEDR First Mediators' Congress 20 November 2003

Palmer, M and Roberts S *Dispute Processes: ADR and the Primary Forms of Decision Making*

Pryles, Michael. 1997 John Keys Memorial Lecture. Assessing Dispute Resolution Procedures (1998) 64 *Arbitration* 106

Roberts, Simon *Toward a Minimal Form of Alternative Intervention* (1986) 11 Mediation Quarterly 25

Roberts, Simon *Mediation in the Lawyers' Embrace* (1992) 55 MLR 258

Roberts, Simon *ADR and the Contemporary Expansion of State Power* paper, IALS WG Hart Legal Workshop 2006: The Retreat of the State: Challenges to Law and Lawyers

Rosenberg, *Contemporary Litigation in the United States* in Legal Institutions Today: English and American Approaches Compared 152 (H.Jones ed.) 1977

Schwerin, Edward W. *Mediation, Citizen Empowerment and Transformational Politics* 1995 Praeger, Westport, Connecticut

Spangler, B. *Problem-Solving Mediation* 2003 Beyond Intractability Knowledge Base Project

Spangler, B. *Settlement, Resolution, Management and Transformation: An Explanation of Terms* 2003 Beyond Intractability Knowledge Base Project

Stone D, Patton B, and Heen S. *Difficult Conversations* (2000) Penguin Electra NY

Von Kumberg, Wolf. The Future for Mediation in Europe (2006) 72 *Arbitration* 62

York, Stephen D, *Preparing Your Client for Mediation* Resolutions issue 17 Summer 1997

Index

---

www.ingramcontent.com/pod-product-compliance
Lightning Source LLC
Chambersburg PA
CBHW060553220326
41598CB00024B/3092